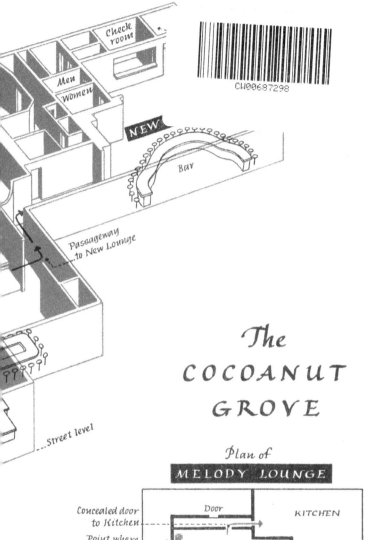

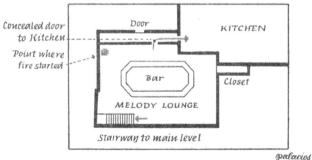

The

COCOANUT

GROVE

Plan of

MELODY LOUNGE

Concealed door to Kitchen

Point where fire started

Door

KITCHEN

Bar

Closet

MELODY LOUNGE

Stairway to main level

palacios

Check room

Men

Women

NEW

Bar

Passageway to New Lounge

Street level

Published in 2023 by Echo Point Books & Media
Brattleboro, Vermont
www.EchoPointBooks.com

First published n 1960 by Frederick Muller, Ltd., London

Holocaust!
ISBN: 978-1-64837-340-4 (casebound)
        978-1-64837-341-1 (paperback)

Cover design by Kaitlyn Whitaker

Cover images—*Front cover:*
The Cocoanut Grove nightclub fire, November 28, 1942,
courtesy of National Fire Protection Association
Back cover (from top):
Two members of an emergency evacuation crew search the
Shawmut Street side of the dining room;
courtesy of World Wide Photos
Fire fighters and servicemen join forces to pass a body through
one of the high windows on Piedmont Street;
courtesy of the Boston Globe
Police and fire department officials inspect the Shawmut
Street side of the club; courtesy of World Wide Photos
A crowd gathered outside Southern Mortuary after the fire;
courtesy of World Wide Photos

FOREWORD

THERE is now nothing on Piedmont Street, in Boston, to indicate that a place called the Cocoanut Grove ever existed.

But the people of Boston know precisely where the Grove stood. Among the generation that was young in 1942, it is difficult to find anyone who did not know somebody who was at the Cocoanut Grove on the night of November 28, 1942.

There are doctors and nurses, bar boys, and cab drivers who will never forget the suffering they saw. There are countless women and men whose lives still reflect the trauma of that night.

For every newspaperman who was then in Boston, the story of the Cocoanut Grove stands as the biggest story he ever covered. Every fireman who helped put out the blaze marks the Grove holocaust as the worst tragedy to which he ever had to respond.

For the Cocoanut Grove fire burned with ferocious swiftness, causing in just twelve minutes the loss of at least 490 lives.

ILLUSTRATIONS

7

1

AT four minutes after ten on the evening of November 28, 1942, Maurice and Jean Levy, of Roxbury, Massachusetts, were distracted from their chat with a couple sitting opposite them in the basement bar of the Cocoanut Grove in Boston.

The room was called the Melody Lounge.

The foursome—the Levys, Corporal Harold Goldenburg, and Florence Zimmerman—sat in the northwest corner of the crowded lounge, some twenty-five feet from a flight of stairs that led to the Foyer above. These stairs were the only public exit from the Melody Lounge.

The room had seldom been busier. It was the last Saturday night of the football season—that afternoon Holy Cross had unexpectedly shellacked a highly favoured Boston College team 55 to 12—and a large portion of the crowd were football fans. Patrons stood three and four deep around the oval bar in the centre of the lounge, and the small tables which filled the remaining space were all occupied. Maurice and Jean Levy sat at one of these tables, facing their friends who were on the zebra-striped settee which ran all the way around the room.

The distraction was minor but amusing. It began just after a sixteen-year-old bar boy named Stanley Tomaszewski brought them their second drink, which they paid for with chits that patrons were required to buy upstairs before being admitted to the Melody Lounge.

At the next table, on the other side of an artificial palm tree that simultaneously provided atmosphere and concealed a ventilating fan, a young man was developing his romance with a petite brown-haired girl snuggled beside him.

He was doing notably well.

The Melody Lounge was as much appreciated for its darkness as for anything else. Tiny bulbs, socketed in cocoanut husks, and indirect lights above the oval bar produced its only illumination. The room was so dark, in fact, that it was not unusual for newcomers to ask if a fuse had blown.

But the darkness did not completely obscure the pantomime in the corner. A yellow bulb on the palm tree threw its feeble beam between the young man and his girl; whenever their heads came together they were brightened by its light.

For the young man, as well as for the Levys, the Melody Lounge had one distinct drawback; it was most pleasant when it was only partially filled. Whenever the crowd exceeded one hundred—and there were nearly twice that number tonight—the smoke tended to linger and become stale, the temperature rose, and patrons were likely to experience an uncomfortable, hemmed-in feeling.

Twice the Levys had to shove themselves more tightly into the corner. Now they were crammed so close to the couple that it was just impossible not to follow the progress of their romance.

Other people were aware of the affair too, for Maurice

Levy saw the girl move away self-consciously when her partner tried to cradle her shoulder in his arm.

It was then that the man noticed the attention on him, and scowled at the seven-and-a-half watt bulb that offended his privacy.

Then he moved.

With the bodily efficiency of a trained athlete, he rose, stepped past his girl toward the corner, and raised one foot to the settee space between her and the palm tree. He shoved himself upward with the other foot and reached between the fronds toward the cocoanut husk. The husk was cut so that its interior would serve as reflector for the bulb; the man gave the bulb a quick twist, then dropped silently back to the floor.

The movement was quick and nearly unobtrusive. In a moment he was back beside the girl, his arm cradling her shoulder precisely as it had before. As he glanced around to assess any reaction to what he had done, a boy in a white bar jacket went by. It was Stanley Tomaszewski on his way to the kitchen with a tray of empty glasses.

The four in the Levy party smiled and resumed their conversation.

Three men tended the oval bar in the centre of the lounge. Emelio Soracco, who worked at the end nearest the romantic couple, glanced toward the corner when it suddenly became a degree darker but was not sure what had attracted his attention. The other two bartenders noticed nothing unusual.

Just then Stanley Tomaszewski returned from the kitchen and squeezed his way between the tables, raising the empty tray over his head to slither sideways through the crowd of people bunched at the bar. He put the tray down at the service plate in the middle of the bar opposite the head bartender, John Bradley.

"The man in the corner just put a light bulb out," Stanley said. "You can't see anything over there now."

Bradley gave a highball its final swizzle and glanced toward the corner. "Who, that soldier?"

"No, the other side," Stanley told him. "A civilian. You can't see him now. He's got his arm around a girl."

Bradley stepped a little way down the bar to look closer, then returned to Stanley. "Listen—be polite about it, understand? Just go over and tell him it's against the law not to have a light there. Then fix it."

Stanley nodded and started for the corner.

"Wait a minute," Bradley said. He leaned over the bar to keep the conversation private. "If he starts any trouble, just walk away, understand? Just turn right around and come back here."

Stanley tried to plan a brief speech as he worked his way back through the crowd. He was pretty sure the man was not drunk, so there was a good chance he wouldn't make a fuss about the light. Stanley absolutely could not afford to get mixed up in any kind of a scene in the club. He was only sixteen—under age to be working at night where liquor was sold. Any unfavourable attention might cost him the job which netted him $2.47 plus substantial tips two nights a week. Stanley's father was not making a living at the time and the money was indispensable at home.

He leaned over and spoke softly as Bradley had told him to do.

"I'll have to put that light on, sir. The law says we have to keep all these lights on for safety."

"Oh, leave it off, kid," the man said. "There's plenty of light here. It was shining right in my eyes."

12

"I'll try to move it, sir," Stanley said.

Then he excused himself to Jean Levy, whose legs partially blocked his access to the corner. She moved, and he squeezed between the corner tables. Stanley had to stare down in the dark for a moment to find a place on the settee for his foot.

The man grumbled, but moved to his left so the girl could make room for Stanley. She picked up the purse which lay on the settee beside her and scooted over far enough to be out of the boy's way.

The Levy party watched as Stanley groped for the bulb. He couldn't find it. He tried with his left hand, using his right to separate some of the fronds that blocked his view. This time he located the bulb, but turned it the wrong way. It came free of its socket and he had to make a quick catch with both hands to prevent its falling to the floor. As he did so, the fronds sprang back over the husk.

Stanley stared into the dark foliage but could not see the socket.

He reached down to the table and picked up a book of Cocoanut Grove matches from the slot of a glass ash tray. He opened the cover, tore out a match, and carefully tucked the cover under its flap.

Then he struck the match.

Stanley cupped his hands around the flame as best he could, but it was an awkward motion. In one hand he held the match book and bulb, in the other the lighted match. But he kept the match safely away from the tree until its first fiery glow burned away. The bulb he stuffed into his breast pocket.

The Levy party was intrigued by what was going on. Maurice watched as Stanley leaned closer to the tree, his right hand still carefully holding the match away from anything it might ignite. Maurice noticed that the hand moved upward as Stanley leaned to the left. The match seemed to ap-

13

proach a single curved blade of a palm leaf, but Levy could not be sure that what he thought he saw was not just a trick of perspective.

Then Stanley carefully moved the match in to illuminate the husk which his left hand had located. The flame did not come within ten inches of anything on the tree. The moment he saw the socket, he blew the match out.

But Maurice Levy was not looking at Stanley's match; he was still studying the palm frond which had seemed to glow a moment before. Maurice thought he saw a flicker on this frond. Then he decided he had not.

With his left hand now on the empty socket, Stanley Tomaszewski gave his full attention to the match stub in his hand. He blew on it again, brought his hand toward the breast pocket containing the bulb, and drew the bulb out. Then he mated bulb to socket.

The corner's faint illumination returned. Stanley, in deference to the man, shoved the husk a little to the left so the light would not inhibit his affair.

Maurice Levy kept watching the palm frond, still uncertain of what he had seen. He was about to ask the bar boy to check the palm when he saw a small puff of light, followed by the appearance of a dark hole in the blue satin ceiling fabric. The peculiar little black hole in the cloth began to widen, its edges curling as it grew.

Then Levy saw the first flame of which he could be absolutely sure. The satin was burning, he realized, and the flame was beginning to edge downward as it ate its way along the cloth.

He reached for Jean's arm to pull her away from the corner.

The Cocoanut Grove was on fire.

Directly above the Melody Lounge was the Grove's spacious Foyer, which during the next few minutes was the scene of a minor drama of its own. The patrons and employees in the Foyer were thus completely oblivious to the confusion developing below.

The central character was a man who had obviously drunk too much. He insisted that he had just been insulted in the Dining Room by a man he described as "my ol' pal."

The Foyer was a long, thickly carpeted hallway. At its centre was a revolving door that led to the Piedmont Street entrance. The drunk had just made his way from the Main Dining Room, at one end of the Foyer, and had moved tortuously past the revolving door to the checkroom.

Ahead of him were two men waiting for their coats. George Hayes, of Quincy, and his friend, Wilbur Boudrey, of Holyoke, had just handed the girl their checks. Their wives, and an unescorted woman in the party, Mrs. Catherine Fallon, were waiting outside the revolving door.

"I gotta get my hat and go home," said the tipsy one. "I just been insulted. An' I don't stay any place where I been 'nsulted."

The hat-check girl, who held both Hayes' and Boudrey's checks in her hand, hesitated. Hayes nodded to her, indicating that for the sake of peace she should get the drunk's things first.

Hayes and Boudrey stepped discreetly away from the man and stood under the apex of the Foyer's vaulted ceiling. They were delayed for about thirty seconds while the man took his hat and coat and weaved out.

In addition to this diversion, the Foyer was busy with a fairly continuous stream of incoming patrons hoping to get tables in the Main Dining Room. Most of them were refused entrance, however, because the Dining Room had been filled to its ordinary capacity for more than an hour.

At about 10.11, when the flames had first begun to cause alarm in the Melody Lounge, all was bustling and gay in the Grove's Main Dining Room. If the outbreak of excitement downstairs did not intrude upon the brief scene in the Foyer, there was even less chance of its being heard in the Dining Room, forty feet farther away.

Waiters were hurrying to set up extra tables on the dance floor in time to seat even more patrons than were already crowded into the room. They had only a few minutes to complete the job before show time.

A vivacious girl named Shirley Leslie was making her way through the crowd with her tray of cigarettes. She was headed for the Terrace, an elevated section of the Dining Room near the entrance from the Foyer.

As she moved, she was greeted here and there by habitués of the Grove. Shirley was almost as well known as Billy Payne, the Grove singer, Mickey Alpert, the Grove bandleader, or Angelo Lippi, the Grove maître d'hôtel. And everyone, it seemed, liked her; "Bunny" Leslie was an attractive fixture of Boston night life.

Bunny usually sat at the back of the Terrace during the floor show, which was due to start at 10.15. She climbed the four steps to the Terrace and smiled as she passed the table at which Western star Buck Jones sat with a party of Boston movie distributors. Then she relaxed in a chair under the spotlight loft and studied the familiar panorama.

The Terrace overlooked the entire Main Dining Room—3,600 square feet of tropical wonderland, ingeniously contrived by Reuben Bodenhorn, then the best-known night club architect in America. Seven tall artificial palm trees, so realistically designed that one half-expected them to sway, flanked the dance floor in front of the bandstand. To the right was the famous Caricature Bar—the longest bar in Boston—forty-eight feet. Behind it were drawings of everyone of fame who had ever entered the club.

Fitted into the base of the stage was a rolling platform that moved out over part of the dance floor at show time and provided a secondary elevated surface from which actors and dancers performed. Above the dance floor, a huge section of the roof was mounted on rollers and track. In summertime it could be rolled back electrically so that patrons could literally dance under the stars.

To the left of the bandstand, a Spanish-tiled roof formed a villa from which customers could see the dance floor. The Villa was elevated above the dance floor by one step. People were forever stumbling on this step, for the plush carpeting was pulled down over its edge deceptively.

Finally, there was the Terrace itself, raised nearly three feet into the Grove's exclusive stratosphere, and reserved for the very best people. It was here that personages of importance responded graciously to their introduction from the bandstand by Mickey Alpert or Billy Payne.

The Main Dining Room, with its fabulous furnishings and chummy atmosphere, was the reason the Cocoanut Grove ranked as the "smartest" of the swank places in Boston.

From the spotlight loft, above Bunny's head a fifteen-year-old "bus boy" (a waiter's helper) named Tony Marra kept his gaze on a table near the stage where Billy Payne, the Grove singer, was sitting with bandleader Mickey Alpert. When the show began, Tony's first assignment would be to put the big spotlight on Billy and the American flag while Billy sang the national anthem.

Tony loved the excitement of the Grove, especially when he had the opportunity to operate the lights for the floor show.

This Saturday night had begun, however, with a major disappointment—the Boston College football team, which had planned to hold a victory party on the Grove's Terrace, had been miserably beaten, and so had cancelled its reservations at the Grove.

Tony's disappointment was only somewhat assuaged when the party of movie men came in. He recognized Buck Jones right away. As bus boy for Jones' table, he had a chance to get close to the Western star, to hear him talk, and even to notice the funny way he had of buttering a piece of French bread, then squeezing it before he ate it.

As Tony crouched in the light loft, feeling his legs going to sleep, he saw the sudden white flash of a photographer's bulb. Lynn Andrews who photographed patrons and sold them prints, had just snapped a picture of a boy and a girl. Tony could see that she was now writing their names on her pad.

The young couple, John and Claudia Nadeau O'Neill, had been married in Cambridge that afternoon and were having a wedding party in the Grove with their best man and their maid of honour.

Tony saw Lynn Andrews look at her watch. There was not enough time left to try to sell another picture, for the Grove's owner, Barnet Welansky, didn't want her shooting flashbulbs after the show began. Lynn headed out of the Grove for the Club Photo Service, a block down the street, to have her pictures developed and printed.

Out in the New Cocoanut Grove Lounge, an addition to the Grove which had been open for just eight days, sat the night police commander of the district, Captain Joseph A. Buccigross. He was not in uniform, although he was on duty.

With him at the table were Garrett H. Byrne, assistant district attorney, and a man whose real name was Moses Levenson but who was known in Boston as "Spider" Murphy.

Byrne was drinking ginger ale. Spider nursed a highball. Buccigross, who was there on business, drank nothing.

It was Buccigross' responsibility, as night commander of South End police, to check personally the three largest night clubs in his area—the Latin Quarter, the Mayfair, and the Cocoanut Grove. Usually he checked them in that order, but tonight he reversed the sequence. He had been on vacation when the New Cocoanut Grove Lounge had opened, and he was eager to see it.

"Barney" Welansky, the Grove owner, was in Massachusetts General Hospital recovering from a heart attack, so Buccigross asked to see Barney's brother, Jimmy, who arrived at the table a few moments later.

Jimmy explained that in order to obtain space for the New Lounge, Barney had bought the two brick buildings which stood between the Grove's Main Dining Room and Broadway. A passageway leading from the Dining Room to the New Lounge was closed to everyone but employees. Barney didn't want to take the chance that "deadbeats" from the main part of the club would duck their checks by slipping into the New Lounge, buying a drink or two, and then leaving through the Broadway door.

Buccigross asked how incoming customers got into the Main Dining Room from the New Lounge.

"They don't," Welansky told him. "We send them around to the revolving door on Piedmont Street."

Buccigross and Welansky continued to chat in the bright new room. Ordinarily they might have wandered through the night club together, but tonight they did not. And there was nothing whatever to suggest that alarm was developing in the usually subdued atmosphere of the Melody Lounge.

The confusion in the Melody Lounge began with a shout from behind the bar.

Emelio Soracco, the bartender, had an excellent view of the corner. He saw the palm tree catch fire only a moment after Maurice Levy had decided it was an illusion. Soracco shouted to John Bradley, and ran toward the tree with a bar towel. Bradley told the third man, Dan Weiss, to watch the bar, then hurried after Soracco.

Stanley Tomaszewski was still unaware that anything was amiss. He had treated the match with utmost caution and had seen it go out safely. Its dead stub was in his jacket pocket.

He was walking away from the corner with his back to the tree when he saw Soracco and Bradley hurrying toward him from the bar. Stanley wheeled and saw that small flames were nibbling along the leaves of the palm tree.

The man who had unscrewed the bulb slipped out from behind his table, pulling his girl along with him. The Levy party left their table and moved toward the standees at the bar, most of whom were watching the flickering tree. But the fire was still so small that most of the people in the Lounge found it amusing. No one but Levy seemed to notice the hole spreading in the ceiling.

While the fire was developing in the Melody Lounge, a man dressed in a dinner jacket was considering whether to jump on to the back platform of Fire Engine 22, which was rolling out of the fire station on Warren Street, a few blocks from the Cocoanut Grove.

Benjamin J. Ellis, head of the Ellis Fire Appliance Company, was probably the most dedicated fire-fighting enthusiast in America. Earlier in the evening, he had been unable to find amusement at two separate dances, so had sought diversion at a place where he was always able to find it—in a fire station. There was no reason that he knew of which had made him choose the station where Engine 22, Ladder 13, a hose wagon, and a rescue unit were stationed.

At 10.15 an alarm box had begun to sound. One . . . five . . . one . . . four. In Ben's mind the pages of the box catalogue rippled quickly. Fifteen-fourteen; Stuart and Carver Streets, South End; borderline call on two districts.

Ben gave one moment of thought to the fact that he had a dinner jacket on. But as the big engine thundered its motor and rolled forward, Ben made his decision.

To hell with the dinner jacket, he said to himself, and he swung up on to the fire engine with Mike Sheehan.

"This is the night of the big one," he shouted to Mike over the crescendo of the siren.

"Yeah!" said Mike, "Every one's the big one for you, Ben."

2

IN the press room at Boston Police Headquarters sat Johnny Sullivan of the *Daily Record*. He faced a squawk box over which calls to police cars could be heard. Nat Kline, covering Headquarters for the *Globe*, was telephoning Metropolitan District Commission Police stations to find out if they had anything doing. Eddie Roth, of the *Herald*, was leafing through the colour magazine of the next day's Hearst paper, the *Sunday Advertiser*. The Boston *Post's* Dick Folsom, newest of the press-room reporters, was reading the teletype for any police messages which ought to be checked.

Nat Kline was keeping the call log for the group. Each time the police dispatcher sent a car somewhere, Nat noted down the call, the division, the time, and the gist of the assignment. Later, when he telephoned around to the police divisions, he could ask about any of the promising items.

At 10.15 the fire alarm tapper began to sound. Nat took a pencil and began noting down each number as it was struck. One . . . five . . . one . . . four. When the number began to repeat he started toward the file of fire alarm box numbers located in the next room.

"Fifteen-fourteen," said Johnny Sullivan, who was the

senior man in the group. "I think that's Stuart and Carver, South End."

"Are you sure?" asked Kline.

"I'm never sure. Look it up," said Sullivan.

Nat flipped the big file cards. "Fifteen-fourteen. Stuart and Carver. Someday I'm going to memorize these things."

He wrote down the number, time, and location of the alarm on his log sheet.

This was the same alarm which had made Ben Ellis decide to jump on the fire engine in spite of his dinner jacket. But it was not an alarm sounded because of the fire in the Melody Lounge. It was only a call for the fire department to do something about a smouldering seat cushion in the front seat of a saloon car parked on Stuart Street, a block and a half away from the Grove.

The small fire in the corner of the Melody Lounge was, meanwhile, flickering brightly. Whether or not it had lighted the ceiling fabric, or had itself caught fire from the ceiling, was now academic. The object was to put it out.

"Get a seltzer bottle!" someone shouted.

"Throw some of that bar rye on it," said someone else. "That's mostly water!"

But Mildred Jeffers, of Wenham, did not laugh. She clutched her husband's hand. "Donald—that fire. And it's so crowded down here!" The enjoyment of celebrating their wedding anniversary was suddenly forgotten. They had repeated the sequence of eleven years before with dinner at the Statler—ordering everything just as they had as bride and groom, including a bottle of champagne. After dining, they had danced a few numbers, then taken a crisp walk over to the Cocoanut Grove for a nightcap in the Melody Lounge.

Now she and Donald watched apprehensively as waiters and bartenders scampered among the tables to throw pitchers of water on the fire, then rushed back to the bar to refill. One waiter swatted ineffectually at the flames with a bar towel.

"Donald!" Mildred repeated. Automatically, she reached for her bag.

"It's all right, dear. They'll put it out."

But the waiters didn't seem to be making progress against the blaze in the tree, and nothing at all was being done about the burning ceiling. "Let's get out of here—now!" Mildred insisted.

"Yes, I think we'd better," said Donald. Taking her hand gently, he pushed back from the table and scanned the room to find the least congested path to the stairs, "Come on," he said.

They skirted the area where bartenders Bradley and Soracco and several waiters were working on the tree. Bradley suddenly called out to the bar boy, "Stanley, help me pull that tree down! That satin above it will burn like mad!"

Soracco was still wildly swinging the bar towel at the burning fronds, while waiters flung pitcher after pitcher of water. But the persistent fire kept breaking out anew.

By now most of the people on the northwest side of the room had begun to move away from the corner. They formed a wall through which the Jeffers could not pass. The Levy party was also halted, for this wall of patrons formed a crescent which blocked everyone who had been sitting between the stairs and the tree.

Although many patrons had risen from their tables, few had yet begun to make a serious effort to leave the room.

About twenty feet away from the burning tree sat a Harvard sophomore, Nathan Greer, and his date, Kathleen

O'Neil, of Brookline. Another Harvard man, Jim Jenkins, sat with them, waiting for his girl to come back from the ladies' room upstairs.

This party saw the first significant attack on the fire; a waiter dashed through an obscure little door in the centre of the wall and reappeared a few seconds later with a fire extinguisher which he had already turned upside down.

"We'd better get out of here," said Jenkins, as they watched the man play the thin stream on the tree. The three students rose from their seats and began moving toward the stairs.

Stanley and John Bradley kept tugging on the tree. The ceiling above it was burning briskly now, showering little scraps of fire down on the tables and floor. Stanley paused to brush out one of the burning brands that had struck his head just as Bradley gave a powerful heave and pulled the flaming tree from its mount.

As the tree came down across John Bradley's shoulder, Stanley looked up to see the flames moving among the billowing satin of the ceiling. When the fire was directly over his head, he jumped up and clutched a wide armful of the burning material and pulled hard. It shredded in his hands, showering him with fire and sparks that singed his hair and seared his face and forehead. The smouldering clump which he held burst into flame. Stanley threw it down quickly, but felt the pain of intense heat on his palms and fingers. Over his head the fire raced on, its fury undiminished by his effort.

Halfway between Stanley and the stairway, another employee of the Grove watched the swiftly developing fire. He was Herbert Schein, a student of veterinary medicine, who worked part time as a bar waiter.

Schein was located in a position to appraise the extent of

the fire far better than Stanley. He remembered that the Melody Lounge was furnished in bamboo, rattan, fibre, netting, and blue satin—all highly inflammable.

He also remembered that the little door to the kitchen was painted and draped so that it was unlikely to be detected by those who didn't know it was there.

Schein considered carefully: If that fire really gets going, there will be a panic. Somebody has got to start these people moving in a sensible way—half of them through the kitchen door, the other half up the stairs.

He looked around. No one was moving, but everyone was standing up. The fire was fanning out from its apex above the tree. When the shreds of burning blue satin began to fall on the heads of patrons, he heard squeals, shouts, and—finally—screams. Somebody had to tell them what to do.

Then Schein lost his opportunity to act. The crowd began to move.

Upstairs on the Terrace sat a Boston newspaperman, slightly bored. His name was Martin Sheridan, and his job at the moment was squiring Buck Jones around to appearances the Western star was making in Boston. Sheridan had put in a big day with Buck, and could be forgiven for not paying closer attention to the baby and family pictures being exchanged by the movie men at their table.

If it had not been for a case of sniffles the Western star had developed while watching the Boston College-Holy Cross fiasco from the Mayor's box that afternoon, Marty and his wife would not have been in the Cocoanut Grove at all. But when Buck begged him to cancel the appearance scheduled for the Buddies' Club over on Boston Common, Marty suggested the party with the movie men at the Grove as a substitute.

Marty was impressed by the size of the crowd in the Cocoanut Grove that night. So much had been said at the football game about calling off the victory party that he half expected the Grove and the city to be deserted in mourning of the Boston College loss.

But even coming down in the cab he had noticed that it was a very busy night in Boston. Four plays occupied the stages of the city's legitimate theatres, and the Casino burlesque house was, oddly enough, host to Salmaggi's popular opera company with its production of *Lucia di Lammermoor*.

The big movie houses were showing *Road to Morocco*, with Hope and Crosby, Abbott and Costello's *Who Done It?*, and *For Me and My Gal*, which featured Judy Garland.

None of this distinguished competition affected Rose La Rose, who was peeling down to the Boston Licensing Board minimum at the Globe Burlesque.

Boston was a serviceman's town on the week ends. Fort Devens, Camp Edwards, the Army Base, the Navy's Fargo Building, Coast Guard Headquarters, Fort Banks, and installations all over New England released thousands of men into the city on two-day passes and liberties.

But no matter how people sought to pass the evening, Marty could observe that November 28 was still Boston College night. Boston was largely Irish and Italian, the two nationalities welded by the huge Roman Catholic archdiocese, second largest in the world. To most of Boston's Catholics, college football meant only one team—Boston College, the Jesuit institution on the Newton-Boston line.

Denny Myers coached the B.C. team that year, using the T formation for the first time in his career. He had the best material B.C. had seen in years, and he made the most of it. The team had torn through its first nine opponents in unbroken victory. Long before the big final game with Holy

Cross, the Catholic college in Worcester, B.C., supporters had bought up every available ticket. Everyone wanted to be there when Boston College rubbed the noses of its arch rivals in the dirt of Fenway Park.

This B.C. team was regarded as so unbeatable that sportswriters were nominating the whole first squad for All-American. It was even suggested that the only team which might beat them was the professional Chicago Bears.

The squad had been chosen to play in the Sugar Bowl and the invitation was to be presented that day. The Sugar Bowl Committee had come to Boston to witness the expected slaughter and had made arrangements for a victory party in the Cocoanut Grove.

But Boston College had lost.

The Denny Myers T, which had bowled over tougher teams, never got off the ground. When the teams switched ends of the field at the quarters, the wind shifted against B.C. three consecutive times. Holy Cross, with mediocre material and a green coach, romped, skipped, passed, and lateralled its way to touchdown after touchdown. The final score was a humiliating 55 to 12 in favour of Holy Cross.

Marty Sheridan and Buck Jones had watched the game from Mayor Maurice Tobin's box. Tobin was a passionate B.C. supporter, and they saw him spiritually crushed when the Sugar Bowl Committee left the stadium before the game was over. It was drizzling then, and Buck was developing his cold, so Marty took advantage of the situation and left to take Buck back to his hotel.

Because of the defeat, the mayor was not in the Grove. But Marty was able to pick up enough conversation on the Terrace and in the Dining Room to realize that a large number of patrons were talking about the game. Their partisan chatter made the room as noisy a place as Marty Sheridan had ever seen. There was too much going on to hear anything—even a scream—from the Melody Lounge downstairs.

But in the Melody Lounge the combined weight of nearly two hundred people had begun to shift and seethe. Tables were overturned and chairs were hurled out of one person's way into the path of another. A man climbed up on the settee to break through one of the small artificial windows. He managed to squeeze his whole trunk into the opening before he found that the window was an illusion which led only to a brick wall.

The fire began to creep along the sides of the room as well as across the ceiling, feeding gustily on the bright leatherette which covered the walls. Everyone in the room was trying frantically to escape now—except one.

Behind the bar, Dan Weiss thoughtfully soaked a bar towel with water, wrung it out slightly, and sat down on the floor. He lowered his head and pressed the wet cloth over his face so that his eyes, nose, mouth, and neck were covered. He leaned against one of the uprights which supported the bar and decided to wait it out.

Stanley Tomaszewski glanced at the patrons pressing hopelessly toward the stairway. No good that way. He ran to the camouflaged door which led to the kitchen. He opened it all the way—shoving it back flat against the wall—so that it would not be swung inward by people squeezing toward it from the other side.

"Through here!" he shouted to those around him. "Into the kitchen!"

Twice Stanley nearly went down in the rush for the door. He helped unscramble people until ten or twelve had passed in the dark hallway beyond. Then he heard their screams and shouts and realized that none of them could know which way to go.

He shoved through the door and groped along the wall, shouting to them to let him show them the way.

Some fifteen feet away were Mildred and Donald Jeffers, who had not got very far from their table. Both had been knocked over in the first ominous shifting of the crowd and were now on their knees, crawling. They barely had time to glance at each other when the faint lights of the Melody Lounge went out completely.

Donald Jeffers crawled ahead of his wife, calling out to her in the dark. He pushed tables and chairs out of their path as he moved, repeatedly checking to make sure Mildred was still near him. He kept bumping into the feet and ankles of others around him.

A thick quilt of black smoke dropped over him so heavily he could feel its hot contact on his back. He did not know where Mildred was, or whether the door was nearby. Donald turned and tried to crawl back, but found there were feet, shoes, moving legs, and crawling forms jammed into the route he had taken. He called out for his wife, but barely heard his own voice. He turned again and continued to grope through the smoky blackness, hoping that somehow she would be all right.

Maurice and Jean Levy reached the base of the stairway at that moment, but they had lost an unbelievable race. When they had started from the corner toward the stairway, the ceiling fire was still ten feet behind them. An odd shifting of the crowd somehow provided them with an open path across the room. They moved forward quickly, confident that they were widening the distance between themselves and the fire.

But suddenly they heard a hissing rush of flame over their heads. It reached the stair well a good ten feet ahead of them and roared upward like a blowtorch. The flames seemed to feed on nothing, neither the material on the stairs nor the slanted ceiling of the stair well. It was as though the air itself were burning over their heads, roaring upward like the flame jets in a gigantic oil burner.

They held on to each other tightly and tried to press into the vortex of people at the base of the stairs.

They heard a shout: "Look out! Damn it, get out of my way!"

It was one of the waiters, who had somehow found room to run a few steps, thus developing enough momentum to hit the crowd on the stairs like a football player. People were knocked left and right, but the waiter kept his feet working. Maurice Levy saw him churn up the stairs, holding his head down beneath the flames and charging heedlessly past the others.

Farther up the stairs the two Harvard boys heard the shout. Nathan Greer looked back just as the charging form hit his chum, Jim Jenkins, knocking him down. Greer and his girl friend, Kathleen O'Neil, stumbled forward, racing to beat the terrible flames.

Behind the bar in the Melody Lounge, Dan Weiss continued to breathe through his wet bar rag and to listen to the sounds of panic. There were now no words he could understand; it was all one continuous shout-scream, the awful cacophony of hysteria. At first, when the fire began to pass over the satin ceiling above him, he had filled a mixing glass with water and—from his sitting position—tossed it up at the flames. But he soon saw the futility of this; the fire now had its own way completely in the room.

Weiss kept soaking the cloth in water and replacing it on his face. The smoke was thick and choking, but he could tell by the difficulty of breathing while wetting his cloth again that his makeshift mask was doing its job. And the closer he held his face to the floor, he found, the easier it was to breathe without pain.

While Weiss was making the most of the air near the floor, the head bartender, John Bradley, was helping about thirty people to pass through a door into a cold smoke-free alley outside. These were the first to escape from the Cocoanut Grove, even though they passed through the door to the kitchen later than the group led by Stanley Tomaszewski.

But Stanley, who did not know the Grove as intimately as Bradley, had led his group to the right, into the complicated passages of the kitchen and storage rooms. Bradley had gone to the left. A few paces that way was a flight of three steps which led to a bolted door. Bradley had shot the bolt back, pulled the door open, then helped his party to safety.

The four leatherette walls of the Melody Lounge burned violently now. And the nine hundred square feet of ceiling, with its voluminous folds of blue satin, were entirely afire. Rattan, fibre, bamboo, and palm leaves fed the flames. The gas produced in the combustion seemed able to refuel itself, so that the air was filled with fire that burned yellow-white and blue-white, depending on whether it was nearer the ceiling or the walls.

Ironically, the desperate patrons struggling to find the stairs could not be guided by the illumination of the flames. The fire seemed phosphorescent, lighting itself but nothing else. Wherever a guiding glow of sorts did occur, it was quickly obscured by the incredibly black smoke that curled and boiled in the air before being sucked toward the steep chimney of the stair well.

The blaze produced a sound that no one in the room had ever heard before—a searing, hissing sound which seemed to move like a whiplash.

About two hours before the fire began, Grove bandleader Mickey Alpert posed with Ezra Stone (second from left) and two other members of the *This Is The Army* cast. In another publicity photo, taken eight days earlier, Bartender William Shea poses with two customers in the New Lounge. Shea died in City Hospital of massive burns. (*Acme Photos*)

The Boston *Globe* obtained these pictures from the camera of Lynn Andrews, the Grove's roving photographer, who took them shortly before the fire. The party above was never identified, but the woman whose face appears in the centre of the picture below was identified by her brother-in-law. Her name was Sadie Levin, and she died in the fire, as did Mr. and Mrs. Theodore Wasserman, the couple at the left. The couple at the right, never identified, was presumed dead. (*Photos by courtesy of the Boston Globe*)

Then the cloud of black smoke thickened and billowed downward toward the floor. It settled over inert forms of men and women still on the bar stools, but unconscious from the fumes they had breathed. It draped over figures sprawled forward across the little tables or doubled over the backs of chairs. It curled downward to shroud the early victims who had slumped on to the settee, some of them blackened and burned. And finally, it whisked along toward the stairway over the backs of the fallen and trodden, already unconscious and dying on the floor.

But outside, still no sign of trouble, save for the frightened knot of people led by Bradley into the kitchen alley.

Over on Stuart Street, which afforded an unobstructed view of the opposite side of the Cocoanut Grove, Ben Ellis, the fire enthusiast in the dinner jacket, was leaning against a big suction hose and idly watching a fire operation.

The men of Engine 22 and Ladder 13 were putting out the smouldering fire in the front seat of the parked saloon.

Mike Sheehan walked past Ben. "This is your big fire, Ben. Think we ought to pull a second alarm?"

Ben chuckled and folded his arms. There would be other big ones, and he would be there. He always was.

3

THE Melody Lounge was literally tucked away from the main part of the club.

To reach it from Piedmont Street, patrons passed through the revolving door into the Foyer, turned to the left, and walked twenty-eight feet to the end opposite the Main Dining Room. There they turned left again, and walked twelve feet more. At this point they were directly opposite an emergency door to Piedmont Street. A flight of thirteen steps to the left of this door led to the Melody Lounge downstairs.

Because the Lounge was physically isolated from the rest of the club, the fire there had remained a grim secret—but only until the flames responded to the updraught on the stairs.

At the moment when the flames began to burst up the stairway, George Hayes and Wilbur Boudrey, who had yielded their priority at the cloakroom to the drunk, were still putting on their coats and chatting about their reasons for having left the Melody Lounge so early.

Their party of five had gone to the B.C.-Holy Cross game that afternoon, and to the Mayfair afterward. Their plan to cap the evening in the Melody Lounge fizzled when Hayes' wife became uncomfortable in the dark and crowded room.

The women, who had not checked their coats, were waiting outside. Hayes and Boudrey were walking toward the revolving door when the first puff of smoke rose from the stair well and eddied around the corner into the Foyer behind them. It was followed by a dart of flame which they did not see.

Hayes and Boudrey saw a Grove employee hurry past them toward the stairs leading to the Melody Lounge, then turn abruptly to dash toward the revolving door. They turned and, for the first time, saw the flames; they responded by rushing toward the door themselves. Boudrey stepped into the door's wedge-shaped opening first, with Hayes to his left and slightly behind. Both squeezed into the same wing. The employee they had followed was crouched at the left of the opening, trying to unfasten the cables that held the door's four wings at right angles.

A crowd quickly converged on the exit, and Hayes and Boudrey pushed forward against one of the panels. The door revolved slightly, then jammed against Boudrey's right foot. He shouted in pain.

Hayes had put his full weight against the door, but when he heard Boudrey's outcry he realized what was wrong—and tried to push the door backward to free his friend's foot. He shoved back as hard as he could, but was unable to move the door.

As the fire raced the length of the Foyer, burning along the vaulted ceiling, terrified fugitives from the Melody Lounge converged on the revolving door and added their pressure to it. Combined with those already at the door, their mass quickly applied so much additional pressure that the men inside could not move in either direction.

A sudden burst of flame flashed close to the door, driving away some of the crowd. With the unexpected relief of pressure, Hayes and Boudrey toppled backward. The door moved slightly and Boudrey's foot was freed.

Hayes pushed forward again on the frame of the revolving door, which he was certain would now turn easily. But it did not. It still stuck fast.

The horde of patrons surged forward again. They were in full panic now. Some of them, a few moments before, had been driven to terror when what had seemed a certain way of escape became a dreadful frustration.

The large steel-covered street door at the top of the stairs from the Melody Lounge had a brass bar stretched across its width some three feet from the floor. Called a "panic" bar, it was designed to open the door in a hurry, no matter which part of the bar was grasped.

The first patrons up the stairs had hit that panic bar. It had not moved. One man had raised his foot and slammed down on the bar, but the bar still did not budge—it had been welded shut. Beneath it, the thick brass tongue of an extra lock gave added assurance that the door could not be opened. Thus had the Grove management, in an effort to insure its profit, made certain that nobody used the emergency door to enter or leave the club without paying the minimum.

The door performed its function tonight, for not a living soul got through it.

The frightened patrons had no choice but to follow the flames into the Foyer and to charge violently toward the exit which they were determined not to be denied. Hayes, seeing the panic in their eyes, shouted in desperation. "Don't push! We can't get it started!"

In that brief glance Hayes happened to notice the face of a very young girl. He saw that her head was held perfectly still, her eyes did not blink, and her mouth did not shape any sound. But her expression was one of worse terror than he had ever seen before.

"Wilbur! We're going out of here!" he said grimly.

Hayes was a big man. He stood over six feet and weighed more than two hundred pounds. He hit the door with all the strength he could muster. It did not move.

"Again, Wilbur—together!"

This time, Hayes let his big fist slam against the plate glass in the door panel. His hand went through the glass and was badly cut. But the wound earned him no more than a small hole in the pane.

Crammed together in the same wing of the door, it was difficult for the two men to co-ordinate their efforts. Hayes' bleeding hand was now trapped at his waist and his face was pressed hard against the glass. Still, he and Boudrey pushed and kicked as best they could.

Outside, under the archway, the three women—Hayes' wife, Mrs. Boudrey, and Mrs. Fallon—watched the frantic struggle. Behind the men they could see the hideous play of fire and smoke around men and women, some of whom they knew must be burning to death.

The mass behind the door suddenly shifted again. Two young engineers from a General Electric plant in Lynn charged at the door just as Hayes and Boudrey reared back for a final assault on the panel.

The four hit the two panels simultaneously and the cables finally snapped. Boudrey was spewed into the street with Hayes as the revolving door spun around. The engineers crashed to the sidewalk with the frame as it broke to pieces. One of them cut his feet badly on the jagged edges of the glass—his shoes had been pulled off during the struggle inside. The other was bleeding profusely from cuts on his face, neck, and arms.

Directly behind George Hayes came a woman who had been selling war bonds to patrons of the Grove. Hayes turned and saw that the front of her dress was on fire. With a quick motion he began to brush out the flames with his hands.

"Stop that! Stop it!" she cried. "You have no right to touch me like that!"

Hayes stepped away from her and turned to watch, helplessly, the terrible struggle inside. Now the circular doorway was filled with frantic people. Hayes saw a woman there, her clothing and hair on fire. She fell forward on to the body of a waiter.

Although Hayes' hand still bled profusely, and Boudrey could not stand on the injured foot, both now realized how lucky they had been to get out.

The waiter, Herb Schein, had been knocked down just as he had felt certain he would be carried through the door by the surge behind him. Now he was pinned to the floor by the burning woman who screamed in agony in his face.

Schein reached up and beat out the tiny flames in her hair with his hand. Then he grabbed the burning fur piece she wore and flung it aside. The woman screamed and kicked in agony. Raising his knee, Schein lifted her so that he could get at her flaming dress. He tore the shoulder strap downward as hard as he could. The burning material shredded away. He kept clawing and tearing until most of her dress was gone. The violent tension he had felt in her body slackened now. She became limp and her screams subsided to moans. He tried to push her to her feet but did not have enough strength to buck the pressure of the crowd behind her. People were trampling over them.

At last Schein managed to push the woman up so that she straddled him. He shoved again and felt her pitch forward, caught up by the crowd. Schein rolled over quickly and scrambled out of the door.

Maurice Levy was heaved out of the door a moment later, but without his wife, Jean. All the way up the stairs, along the passageway, and through the Foyer, he had resolutely held her by the shoulders in front of him, guiding her toward the revolving door. He had used his back as a barrier against the crowd. He was determined that, if the pressure became too great, at least he might have a chance to push her out.

But in the last seconds, when the heaviest weight of the crowd bore on him and he had been sure he and Jean would be forced through the door together, the direction of the pressure had suddenly changed, and Jean had been snatched away. He saw her taken up by the surging mass while he was shoved helplessly through the door. In his last glimpse of her, she was headed down the Foyer toward the entrance to the Main Dining Room.

A similar shifting of the crowd, at the opposite end of the Foyer, caught Nathan Greer and Kathleen O'Neil. They had just come up from the Melody Lounge, where they had tried to wait until Jenkins, knocked down by the waiter, regained his footing. But the wild horde had pushed forward so insistently that Greer and Kathleen were forced to dash up the last few steps in order to keep their balance.

When they started toward the Foyer, they felt the hot blast of fire surge over their heads. Nathan took Kathleen's hand and held it tight. Then they crouched under the flames and hurried ahead of the crowd.

But when they came abreast of the cloakroom, Kathleen suddenly stopped. "My coat . . ."

Greer stared at her in amazement.

The delay proved crucial. Greer felt himself shoved violently forward. He tightened his grip on her arm and felt her fingernails dig into his wrist, but she could not hang on. Their hands separated and Greer, unwillingly freed of her weight, shot forward like an arrow from a bow.

He found himself jammed into the circular doorway among those struggling to escape. By working his legs and shoulders mightily he was able to wedge forward little by little. He was suddenly spun around, and shoved toward the opening back-first. Beside him he saw a man fighting desperately to free his hands, trapped at his sides, so that he could brush out the fire in his hair.

Greer was twisted around again and thrust sideways through the door. He felt the cold air from outside suddenly stab his face as the monstrous pressure on his body abated. He jumped aside and peered back anxiously to see if he could locate Kathleen.

Near Nathan Greer, outside the door, was a young girl from the North End. She had been one of the first to escape —she had gone safely through the revolving door just as the first wisp of smoke appeared in the Foyer. Now, watching with horror the pandemonium inside, she could not put out of her mind what a Grove employee had done as people started to flee the club.

He had tried to block the exit by holding up both arms. "Nobody gets out of here till he pays the check!"

4

IT took less than a minute for the flames, after shooting up the stairs from the Melody Lounge, to reach the ventilating fan near the entrance to the Dining Room. But during most of that minute, while scores were fighting for survival in the Foyer, the gay patrons in the big Dining Room were ignorant of danger. Because of a curtain which hung at the doorway, few of them could see into the Foyer.

In the middle of the Dining Room, some thirty feet from the entrance, Marion Bizzozero of Quincy sat with her husband and a party of friends. Their table flanked the right-hand edge of the dance floor. Marion's only concern, at the moment, was that she was sitting too far from her husband, who was some fifteen feet away. The Bizzozeros had entertained the others at an after-the-game cocktail party in their home, so it was more or less natural that they continue their roles of host and hostess by heading the table. They were thus the only couple in their party not sitting together.

Across the room, on the left-hand side of the dance floor, sat Jake Slate, a South Shore tobacco dealer who earlier had caused the drunk in the Foyer to claim he had been insulted. Slate's mood that night was not convivial. He was seated on what he regarded as the "wrong" side of the club. The table was too close to the stage, he grumbled repeatedly, and the service was "terrible." He told his wife, Ethel, that he could see no good reason why such frequent customers as they should receive such shoddy treatment. Ethel tried to quiet him several times in deference to their guests, who were enjoying themselves, but Jake remained audibly displeased. When the drunk had come to their table and offered to buy a round, Jake bluntly told him to go home.

At a table between Slate and the bandstand, Mickey Alpert and Billy Payne were waiting to start the floor show. But the waiters were still putting up extra tables at the other end of the dance floor, and the show could not begin until they finished.

As Mickey slumped in his chair he said, "Billy, I'm tired. I'm really bushed."

"Me too," said Payne. "I think I caught cold in that wet stadium. I wish those waiters would hurry so we could start."

Mickey reminded him that Buck Jones would have to be introduced during the show. "Maybe we ought to go up and say hello now," Mickey said.

Then, suddenly, both men heard a distant shout they interpreted as "Fight!"—as did at least twenty others in the room.

The cry, of course, was "Fire!" but the shady history and questionable reputation of the Cocoanut Grove were such that a free-for-all was a more likely threat.

The Grove had been opened as a legitimate enterprise in 1927 by Mickey Alpert and his brother, George, who later became president of the New Haven Railroad. But early in the thirties they sold the club to Charles "King" Solomon, an underworld figure who operated it as a plaything, deriving his main income from bootlegging and other rackets. Shortly after taking over the Grove, King Solomon was ignominiously shot to death in the men's room of the nearby Cotton Club.

Barney Welansky and Herbert Callahan had been Solomon's attorneys. Callahan was then building a reputation as one of the country's leading criminal lawyers, so Barney handled most of the firm's business affairs, including the settlement of Solomon's estate.

Solomon's widow allowed Welansky to take title to the Grove. Perhaps he got it free, perhaps he paid cash. Whatever transpired, no exchange of money was recorded. And, though Barney soon made the Grove the most profitable night club in the city, Solomon's widow never complained.

The manner in which Barney operated his club may also have contributed to the fact that the word "Fire!" was misinterpreted.

Barney sensed that the public was intrigued by the Grove's former Prohibition and gangland reputation, so he did not obliterate that atmosphere entirely. He was shrewd enough to realize that his club must avoid the ire of the community's powerful religious leaders, but he was just as aware that the suggestion of naughtiness had unique drawing power.

So he created a dark and mysterious Melody Lounge, but he assiduously refused to serve drinks to minors. He imparted a worldly atmosphere to his Main Dining Room, but he removed all smut from the floor shows. He tolerated, and even featured, the presence of figures associated with the underworld, but in no way let their presence offend patrons from Newton, Cambridge, or Milton. Frequently this delicate balance was upset by a scuffle, but Barney's employees were trained to quell such outbreaks quickly.

Now, while patrons drank and laughed together in Barney's swank Main Dining Room, an almost perfect combustion cycle was taking place in the Foyer. The hot, partially

43

burned gases from the fire in the Melody Lounge had been forced up the throat of the stair well. As they came into the corridor, they mixed and churned with oxygen-rich air. Still under pressure, and gaining heat by the second, they expanded into the vaulted Foyer. The large ventilating fan over the Caricature Bar at the opposite end of the Foyer sucked this roaring fire forward so that it spat like a blowtorch toward the Dining Room entrance.

No one can estimate accurately how long it took the fire to race the length of the Foyer. But it was during this brief period that the shouted alarm was misinterpreted and those in the Dining Room began to react.

One of the first was Tony Marra, the bus boy in the spotlight loft. He heard the shout, saw the reflection of a flash near the Foyer entrance, and immediately concluded that gangsters, most likely armed with machine-guns, were shooting up the place.

Tony leaped from the loft to the Terrace floor, vaulted over the iron railing, and ducked down the stairway to the kitchen.

Mickey Alpert and Billy Payne responded to the shout almost as quickly. Long experience in the night club business had taught them to anticipate any conflict between patrons, and to break it up at once. Both jumped up from chairs and hurried toward the Foyer.

As they scampered between crowded tables, they passed several parties who had already got to their feet. These patrons had responded to a symptom of the fire which Billy and Mickey did not see—a puff of pinkish smoke that eddied lazily near the ceiling, so thin that it could be discerned only from certain angles to the ceiling lights. The smoke gave no inkling whatever of the blast of fire coming behind it.

The two entertainers suddenly reached a point in the Dining Room from which they could look through the entrance and see that the Foyer was bright with flame. Both stopped abruptly, aghast at the sight.

Then the fire made its gargantuan entrance into the room.

First came a fast-moving puff of black smoke. A rosy dart of flame shot along the ceiling fabric for ten or twelve feet. It was instantly followed by a massive ball of flame—bright, noisy, and terrifying. It seemed to burn in the air, without need of fuel. Suddenly everyone in the room was in motion, desperately seeking escape.

Billy and Mickey were driven backward by patrons nearer the fire. Both shouted, trying to establish order, but without success. They had no choice but to turn and run toward the kitchen stairway, where Tony Marra had made his escape.

Marion Bizzozero had popped an oyster cracker into her mouth precisely at the moment when the flames appeared. As those at her table jumped up in alarm, the cracker caught in her throat and she began to cough uncontrollably. Before she could clear her throat, her friends and others nearby began to move toward what seemed the best exit—a narrow door at the left of the stage.

Marion was seized with fear, and wanted urgently to call out to her husband. But she could not control her coughing. As she was swept into a stampede across the dance floor, she looked for him in vain. Then the lights went out, and she could recognize no one. Terrified, retching as much now from the smoke as from the cracker, Marion could barely keep her balance as she was propelled toward the narrow door which led somewhere backstage.

Jake Slate and his wife, at that moment, were already close to the door toward which Marion headed. But they were caught in a more tightly packed crowd than she, and could only inch their way along. Jake clung to Ethel's hand and tried to help her fight against the mounting pressure within the fan-shaped group. Several times he tried to change the direction in which they moved, but each attempt failed. He was beginning to feel dizzy from the sweet-smelling gas the fire produced. He decided that all he could do was to hang on to Ethel's hand and push blindly toward the door.

Some twenty feet behind Jake Slate, a concerted assault was being made on another exit—the closed double door located in the centre of the Shawmut Street wall. One of the men trying to open it was John J. Walsh, Civil Defence director of Boston.

Walsh had understood the cry of fire distinctly, and had seen the first cloud of smoke against the ceiling. He had risen from his chair under the tiled Villa roof on the Shawmut Street side of the Dining Room and spoken calmly to his friends: "There seems to be a fire. Let's all leave quietly. Don't even bother with coats and hats."

With no excitement or confusion, Walsh had led his party to the double door, reaching it just as the lights went out. The exit was equipped with inside screens, which Walsh opened and swung back against the walls. But the door itself was locked. Walsh gathered his party around him, then he and several men began to batter the door with their shoulders.

Far across the room, at the entrance from the Foyer, head-waiter Frank Balzerini shouted urgently to the club's wine steward: "Run like hell and open that Shawmut Street door!"

It was the wine steward, Jack Goldfine, who had tried desperately to uncouple the cables on the revolving door. His hand still throbbed from having been gouged by some man's heel. It was also Goldfine who had shouted the alarm, although he had intended it only for Balzerini. Now, as Goldfine hurried toward the tricky double door, Balzerini made a

Herculean effort to quell the aimless rush of terrified patrons around him.

Goldfine was suddenly knocked down and shoved under a table in the dark. Balzerini had better luck in controlling the panic. By shouting incessantly, by pushing, blocking, and badgering patrons, he finally achieved command of a cluster of people just below the Terrace. He ordered them to move toward the double door. They responded so overwhelmingly that he was caught up in their sudden surge.

Just then Walsh's group, up ahead, was joined by another, led by Frank Accursio. Accursio, a Melody Lounge waiter, had escaped from the burning lounge by crossing the kitchen and climbing the stairs to the Dining Room. He had realized, by the composure of the first patrons he saw upstairs, that he had beaten the fire. There had been time for him to alert a group of patrons sitting near the stair entrance and lead them to the Shawmut Street door.

Accursio arrived just as the safety director and his friends knocked open one side of the door with their shoulders, then stepped back to let some of the women pass through first. Accursio, propelled by those behind him, scooted through the door and on to the sidewalk without even realizing the door had been a problem.

Walsh was pushed out next, but stayed near the door to pull people through. Balzerini, still pushed along by the crowd from the centre of the room, tried to stop when he reached the exit, but was shoved outside. The headwaiter fought his way back against the stream of fleeing patrons until he was finally able to unlatch and open the other side of the double door. Then he forced his way back into the club for another attempt to organize the crowd.

Marion Bizzozero, at that moment, stumbled and fell to her knees in the narrow doorway at the left of the stage. She expected to be trampled immediately, but instead was pushed from behind in such a way that she was suddenly lifted to her feet. She hurried forward, following those ahead. A few seconds later she passed safely through a Shawmut Street service door to which the backstage passage led.

Although Marion had been seated more than thirty feet farther away from the narrow door than Jake and Ethel Slate, she had reached and passed through it before they had moved more than a few feet.

Jake doubted now that he would ever reach the door. The strange gas had weakened him considerably and he was barely able to move. As drowsiness overtook him he suddenly realized how dangerous the situation was. He became convinced he would die there unless he could force himself to keep pushing. When Ethel began to sag on his arm, he tried heroically to muster enough strength to shake her back to awareness. But he could not do it. He found himself soothed by the sweetness of the smell. Slowly he let himself succumb to the pull of Ethel's weight. Completely at peace, he went to sleep beside her on the floor.

The first blast of fire inside the Main Dining Room had burned a brilliant red—the result of hot gases from the Foyer igniting on contact with the oxygen in the Dining Room. These flames had quickly set afire the hundreds of yards of blue satin on the ceiling and the leatherette on the walls. The wild fire achieved its command of the room just as the lights went out—probably in less than a minute. With the darkness, panic raged beyond any possible control.

Those on the Terrace were hopelessly trapped. They were three feet closer to the hot gases billowing down from the burning ceiling, and they were hemmed in by a wrought-iron railing.

The Piedmont Street side of the Grove as it burned. The revolving door, where Hayes and Boudrey made their escape, is beneath the marquee. (*Wide World photo*)

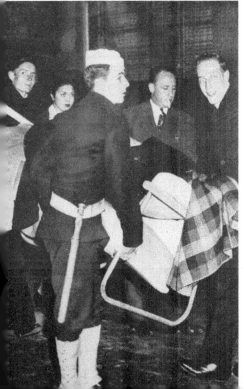

So large was the number of injured and dead that these rescuers had to use a lounge chair, from the nearby Club Mayfair, as a stretcher to evacuate victims. *G l o b e* photographer William Ennis took this picture at about 10.40 p.m., before the evacuation effort was fully mobilized.

(*Left*) Western star Charles "Buck" Jones posed with this patient of Boston's Children's Hospital on the morning of November 28, 1942. It was the last known photograph taken of Jones before he was mortally burned in the Cocoanut Grove that night. (*Wide World photo*)

(*Below*) A priest administers conditional absolution while a survivor attempts to see if the victim is someone he knows. (*Photo by William Ennis*)

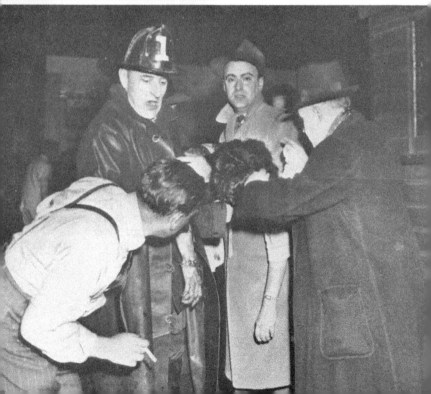

When the superheated smoke—now dense black—reached the wide-open door on Shawmut Street, it ignited and blasted backward over the heads of the victims on the Terrace.

Bunny Leslie, the vivacious cigarette girl, slumped to the Terrace floor, burned and unconscious.

Buck Jones fell at the corner of the Terrace. Newspaperman Marty Sheridan and his wife, Constance, were so quickly overcome by fumes that even though they had been sitting side by side, he never knew where she was as consciousness receded.

The youngest guest at the Cocoanut Grove that night, fifteen-year-old Eleanor Chiampa, was also overcome by fumes on the Terrace. Her brother, Benjamin, and his wife, whose guest Eleanor had been at the B.C. game and at dinner in the Grove afterward, fainted and fell to the floor near her.

Headwaiter Frank Balzerini was directly below the Terrace stairs when the smoke exploded. He had worked his way back from the Shawmut Street door, and was struggling desperately to establish order among the fugitives. The fire swirled around him, and he sank to the floor with his dinner jacket ablaze.

5

DURING the few minutes the fire had taken to spread through the Dining Room, the crowd had formed into five distinct groups, each rushing toward an exit spotted just before the lights went out or remembered from past experience.

As the five groups moved, their numbers constantly decreased. Some were struck by the flames, and either burned to death or fell in pain and shock. Others were overcome by the strange gas. Despite the panic, only a few suffered injuries attributable to the stampede.

The fastest-moving of the five packs was the one that had headed toward the passageway to the New Lounge. Most of these people came from the area surrounding the Caricature Bar. One man, however, had started from the Foyer. He had jumped upon the forty-eight-foot bar and raced the whole length of its surface, then jumped off the end near the passageway.

The corridor to the New Lounge was wide and clear, and the fugitives in it were able to move swiftly. A few of them stumbled over three unexpected steps which led up to the level of the New Lounge buildings, but they regained their footing before they could be trampled.

The second group had inched slowly toward the narrow door at the left of the stage. Because they converged on this door from all sides, much of their pressure was exerted against one another, exposing them longer to the poisonous fumes. The door was only wide enough for one person to pass through at a time, and the dark corridor beyond was complicated by stairs and turns that further delayed the exodus. Only about half of the patrons striving to reach this door actually got through, and the majority of these apparently came from the right-hand side of the room.

While patrons in this second pack were passing through the corridor, a strange and urgent struggle was taking place not far from them on the bandstand. There, three musicians were barred from escape by a bass drum and a set of traps that blocked the exit from the stage.

The band had been waiting for the show to start, when the fire reached the Dining Room. The first to see it was Romeo Ferrara, a saxophone player, who gave the alarm to the others.

Bernardo Fazioli, the musical director and violinist of the group, quickly took charge. He told the men to move off the tiered stand in an orderly sequence—brasses from the elevated rear rows first, then the saxes and rhythm from the front and side. Most of the musicians got through the stage exit without difficulty, descending into the same corridor that patrons entered after passing through the narrow door at the left of the stage.

Al Maglitta, the drummer, noticed that all except Fazioli were carrying their instruments. He debated a moment. A set of traps was a big investment; they would certainly be ruined unless he got them out. He lifted the cumbersome bass drum with its traps and headed toward the exit.

Fazioli had lingered for several seconds in a futile attempt to locate his violin in the dark. Then he followed. Just ahead of him was a saxophone player named Al Willette. Willette had been delayed when he stumbled into one of the bulky plywood music stands which decorated the stage.

Maglitta, lugging the drum in the dark, did not gauge the width of the door accurately. The bass drum somehow wedged into it and stuck fast. Willette called to him, "Get going, Al! We've got to get out of here!"

"I can't! I'm stuck!" said Maglitta.

By then the smoke was agonizing in their throats. Willette and Maglitta shoved and tugged at the instrument, but they couldn't move it forward or back.

Fazioli joined them, and finally the drum came free. It rolled through the doorway and bounced down the stairs into the corridor.

But it had delayed the musicians too long. They had inhaled too much of the smoke and gas filling the room. All three fell unconscious in the passageway.

While the musicians were struggling with the drum, the third of the five fleeing groups was making good headway. This group consisted of patrons who hurried toward the wide exit on Shawmut Street, where Walsh and his friends were helping people to escape. Most of those seated near the door had passed through it without delay, so that those who followed from tables nearer the dance floor were able to move without serious hindrance. The exit on Shawmut Street seemed their best hope of escape. Their only problem was to find a route through the dark.

The fourth group, smallest of the five, included those who had been sitting near the Terrace, within sight of the kitchen stairway. It was led by Mickey Alpert and Billy Payne, who had been forced in that direction by the crowd. As they descended the stairs, they were momentarily halted by fugitives from the Melody Lounge who had crossed the kitchen and were now trying to reach the Dining Room. After a few seconds those coming up realized that the fire had beaten them, and returned to the smoke-filled kitchen. The stairway was freed for those coming down.

The most tragic of all the panic-stricken packs was the one that tried to enter the Foyer. Most of these people automatically headed for the main exit when the first cry went up, not knowing that flames were soon to appear above their heads. One move toward the Foyer, in the ensuing panic, had been enough to commit them irrevocably. The fire struck them head on. Black smoke-filled gas rolled over them, igniting with a dull explosion on contact with fresh air.

These patrons also bucked the frantic tide of fugitives who had been halted by the revolving door and had run in desperation toward the Dining Room. The two hysterical hordes met in the Foyer about twelve feet from the exit. There they fused in a futile attempt to escape.

The fire blazed around them; the air was filled with searing gas. By now their minds were not functioning; only animal instincts kept them pushing, fighting for priority in the pack.

They could not know it, but they were struggling violently only to pile themselves up in death before a doorway through which no living soul could now pass.

The sticky, sweet smell filled their nostrils, and black-brown smoke choked their throats and lungs. During each few seconds that they struggled in the Foyer, their numbers were winnowed by the score. Most of them simply lost consciousness and slipped to the floor to become the death barrier for those behind them.

The last frantic effort of the dying was their attempt to climb over the dead, but they went only far enough so as to arrange incredibly neat stacks of corpses seven and eight deep.

No one in the tragic fortress of blackened flesh got closer than ten feet from the doorway.

While hundreds of victims were struggling and dying in the Dining Room, Foyer, and Melody Lounge, a group of chorus and show girls were expressing their sorrow over the possible fate of some stray dogs housed in an Animal Rescue League shelter at Stuart and Carver Streets, about fifty yards from the Grove.

These Cocoanut Grove girls, costumed and playing fantan in the second-floor dressing room over the New Lounge on Broadway, were idly waiting for the show to begin.

One of them, Connie Warren, was at the front window from which she could look out and see a cluster of fire engines and a wisp of smoke. The smoke issued from the burning seat cushion in the saloon parked on Stuart Street, but Connie could not see the car.

"Oh, those poor dogs!" said "Pepper" Russell, a brunette dancer from Mattapan. "They could burn alive in those cages!"

The other girls continued their game while Connie described the action on Stuart Street. No one had any inkling of the pandemonium below.

The girls had begun their game when they learned that the show would not start on time. Earlier, Pepper Russell had gone downstairs and seen the waiters setting up extra tables on the dance floor. She had reported this to the chorus line captain, Jacqueline Maver, who went down to see how much space was left for the dance routines. When Jackie saw that the new tables were not yet occupied, she went back to the dressing room and told the girls there would be a delay.

The girls were engrossed in their card game when, suddenly, Charlie Mikalonis, a waiter, burst into the room.

"Girls! There's a bad fire downstairs!" he exclaimed. "You can't get out this way—it's packed! Follow me!" He crossed the room, opened a window leading to the adjoining roof, and climbed out, not waiting to see if anyone followed.

Mikalonis had good reason to hurry, for he had reached the dressing room from the area of most violent panic— the Foyer. Somehow he had found a route through the frantic hordes in the Dining Room and made his way upstairs. Now, outside the window, he raced along the roof's parapet until he spotted a clear space in the parking lot below. Then he jumped twenty-two feet to the pavement, landing without apparent injury.

But the girls did not follow him. Jackie Maver rushed to the door, and most of the others scurried after her.

They could hear strange sounds coming from the club— sounds of glassware breaking, tables scraping over the floor, and, from the corridor below, the screams of those trying to get to the service door on Shawmut Street.

The stairway was dark and smoky. But Jackie could tell that the corridor below was packed with people scrambling to get out. It was only a step or two, however, from the bottom of the stairs to the door. If she and the girls hugged the wall, they could probably avoid being hurt by the crowd.

Despite her own mounting fear, Jackie asserted her authority. "Girls, let's make a line. Everybody put your hand on the shoulder of the girl in front of you. I think you'd better put your other hand over your mouth—the smoke is bad out there. And stay close to the wall—I think we can get out through the service door."

"But that door won't be open!" cried one of the girls. "It's always locked!"

"The firemen will open it!" Jackie assured her. "That's the first thing they do!"

"The firemen aren't here!" Connie Warren protested. "They're over at the Animal Rescue League—I saw them!"

"They're here!" Jackie insisted. "Now let's go!"

There were five of them in the line: Jackie, Pepper Russell, Peggy Colligan, Eleanor Gale, and Connie Warren. Two stayed behind.

Hugging the wall, covering their mouths, and holding one another's shoulders, the girls moved down the steep stairs. As Jackie had hoped, they reached the street unscathed.

In the adjacent building, on a similar flight of stairs, a most unexpected episode was taking place. It had begun with a cry wholly foreign to the atmosphere of a night club,

"My babies! My babies!"

A man and a woman rushed up the stairs to a flat on the same level as the dressing room, but separated from it by a brick wall. They hurried into the bedroom, paused a moment, then raced downward to the street.

When they came out, each was carrying a child. The woman held a three-year-old girl, wrapped tightly in a blanket. The man carried a smaller child whose head he cradled on his shoulder.

The couple were Mr. and Mrs. Leslie Tracy. The younger child was a two-year-old boy named Richard. The girl, Leslie, had been named for her father, who worked as handyman for the Grove. When Barney Welansky had bought the buildings for the New Lounge, he let Tracey move his family into an apartment above, where they lived rent free.

The Tracy children, certainly the least likely of victims to flee a burning night club, were hardly exposed to a puff of smoke as their parents carried them out.

6

ONE of the most incredible facts of the Cocoanut Grove disaster is that when death was complete in the Melody Lounge and the Foyer, and rapidly increasing its toll in the Dining Room, there still remained several seconds in the New Cocoanut Grove Lounge before anyone there became aware of the fire.

Jimmy Welansky, still chatting with Police Captain Buccigross, was interrupted at about 10.19 by a young girl whom Buccigross recognized as a Grove employee.

"Mr. Welansky," she said, "you'd better come right away. There's a fire in the lobby."

She had barely finished her announcement when smoke from the Foyer exploded into the New Lounge. Welansky and Buccigross started toward the passageway just as a pack of survivors appeared under the incoming smoke. It took only a glance to forecast what would happen next.

"Take it easy," Welansky shouted, holding up both hands.

"Slow down—slow down!" Buccigross called.

But they, the girl, and the customers near them were hit head on by those at the front of the pack. In seconds they found themselves being hurled backward toward the Broadway door.

Buccigross kept shouting for order and trying to slow down the rush. But these people were fugitives from the hideous fire in the Dining Room, and they were too terrified to be controlled. The police captain was knocked to the floor and trampled by dozens of feet. When he managed to get up, he was again shoved brusquely toward the door.

At his side now was Roberto Garcia, an entertainer, who had been performing on a stage back of the bar. When the black smoke had billowed in from the passageway, Garcia shouted a warning to his wife, Melissa, who danced at the other end of the stage. He jumped to the bar and turned to help her, but she had already disappeared in the smoke. Garcia then jumped to the floor, still searching for his wife. But he was caught up in the throng that surged toward the front door, and became, unwillingly, the first to reach it. When he grabbed the doorknob he felt a powerful electric shock; he could not let go because people were pressing behind him.

"Push back!" he screamed.

But the electric current stopped.

When the patrons near Garcia moved away, he was able to pull back the door and pass through a ten-foot vestibule to the exit on Broadway.

Buccigross remained inside a moment longer, pinned against the wall by the crowd trying to squeeze into the entry. He could see that another group of people were clustered around the cloakroom counter at his right. Incredulous, Buccigross realized that some of them were actually stopping to see if they could get their coats.

"Come on!" he ordered. "You've got to get out of here!" In response to his shout, he was pushed through the vestibule and on to the street.

A block and a half away, Ben Ellis watched the firemen as they methodically stowed their equipment back on the fire truck. Even though it had been only a smouldering cushion, the men had gone through the full routine of connecting hoses and putting their apparatus into position for action, as they were trained to do.

"Why don't you do something about that fire over there?"

Ben glanced up and saw that it was a young woman who spoke. Her arm pointed toward a street off Broadway whose name did not immediately occur to him. Along the edge of a low building there he saw thin curls of smoke eddying out of the eaves. He began to run towards Broadway, scanning the building for its name.

He had gone only a short distance when he recognized the street. Shawmut, of course! Far down its length he saw a sign, its letters made wispy by the rising smoke: "Dine and Dance. COCOANUT GROVE. Visit The Melody Lounge."

The smoke did not then indicate a serious fire to Ben. His first assumption was that grease had probably caught fire in the kitchen flue. But he continued running as fast as he could.

Also running toward the Grove, but at a right angle to the path Ben was taking, was a taxi driver named Sam Meyers who had been waiting for a fare nearby. As he approached the Broadway door Meyers saw that it was blocked by a florid, heavy-set man. Facing the man were several patrons, obviously trying to get past him on to the street. But each time one of them pushed forward out of the entry, the man swung his fist violently and drove the victim back. He was shouting, irrationally, "Edith! Where are you?"

Then a sailor in the doorway lunged toward the man, ducking under the fist. The cab driver jolted him from the other side. They jockeyed him out of the doorway just as Ben Ellis arrived.

The small entry was crammed with people scrambling for the outer door. The panic struck Ben as ludicrous—a small kitchen fire, and these people trampling each other to get away from the smell.

He stepped into the vestibule and grabbed someone's hand. "Here we go!" he said gaily. "Just like olives in a bottle. Get the first, and the rest come easy!"

Ben pulled the man through, then a young girl, then another. He deliberately spun them a little, confident that they would pick up the spirit of his impromptu game.

But no one laughed, and in the next instant Ben saw why.

The entire ceiling was covered with a blanket of soot-coloured smoke. The smoke was eddying swiftly toward the door, obviously pushed along by a high degree of pressure.

Ben Ellis had been to more than 30,000 fires in his lifetime. He knew that the black smoke was hideously combustible, that as soon as it reached a fresh supply of air . . .

Like a match touched to an enormous row of gas jets, the smoke ignited!

There was a rumbling, muffled explosion. The black smoke near the ceiling brightened into yellow fire.

The time was 10.20. Into the next few minutes were compressed, in every part of the club and at several places far removed from it, hundreds of acts of violence, desperation, and sacrifice.

Two blocks away an off-duty fireman, Dennis Sullivan, was getting ready for bed. He poked his head out of his apartment window to see if he could locate the engines he had heard several minutes before. As he looked toward Broadway, he saw a ladder truck parked on Stuart Street. He could also see smoke rising from the Grove.

Instantly, Sullivan guessed that this might be one of those

situations most dreaded by firemen: a second fire occurring close to one for which an alarm had already been sounded, but not close enough to be seen immediately by the fire crews who respond. Witnesses, who would ordinarily ring an alarm for the second fire, see or hear the apparatus and assume the alarm has been rung.

Sullivan shouted to his wife as he began pulling on his clothes. "Call in an alarm! Tell 'em it's Piedmont and Broadway! I think the Cocoanut Grove is on fire!"

At that moment District Fire Chief Daniel Crowley walked toward Lieutenant John R. Coleman, who was supervising the loading of fire equipment on to Engine 22. When Coleman saw his superior approaching, he turned to face him. Crowley's back was toward Broadway and the Shawmut Street side of the Grove.

"You can sound the 'all out' and go back whenever you're ready, John. I'm going . . ."

"Good God! Look!" Coleman shot his arm across Crowley's shoulder, pointing toward Shawmut Street. Crowley wheeled and saw the smoke rising from the eaves of the Cocoanut Grove. Both men dashed along Stuart Street until they reached a point from which the Broadway and Shawmut sides of the night club were visible.

In a glance, Crowley saw enough to support an extreme decision. "Get to that box!" he told Coleman. "Skip the second alarm! Sound a third on fifteen-twenty-one and check back with me!"

While Chief Crowley ran toward the Grove, a fifty-six-year-old woman was dying for the sake of $2,200 in cash that belonged to Barney Welansky. Katherine Swett, the cashier, was slumped over a desk near the stairway in the kitchen. Several employees had tried to persuade her to leave, but she was afraid to go outside carrying so much cash and did not dare to leave it behind. So she stayed at her post and died of suffocation.

A Panamanian girl named Monica Files groped past Katherine's desk with her husband. The couple had just come down the stairway from the Dining Room where Monica had witnessed a pathetic scene—an Army Lieutenant, frustrated in several attempts to break through the crowd, had sat down on the floor and begun to sob uncontrollably. Monica had also seen men hurling chairs and tables recklessly, knocking over women, and stamping over the fallen and injured. There were only a few such reckless men, but their actions were so menacing that Monica and her husband had risked delay in order to avoid them. Monica was still very frightened, but she felt a moment of pride and gratitude as her husband guided her through the smoky basement in search of a door.

Across the room from the couple, Donald Jeffers, who had lost his wife in the Melody Lounge, steeled himself against a scream that he knew was coming. Jeffers was huddled in a darkened walk-in refrigerator. He had found the entrance to it while crawling along the kitchen floor, as had a waiter who assured him the refrigerator would be a safe place to escape the smoke. With them was a woman who repeatedly screamed for help. Jeffers tried to prepare himself for each outburst, but was never quite set for the sudden shock of her voice when it bounced at him from the cold wooden walls.

Also in the refrigerator was a young woman down on her knees. In a tight, throaty voice she was rapidly reciting prayers. She paused only when she took a breath, which Jeffers could hear her clutch into her throat as though it were to be her last.

As Jeffers listened to the two frightened women, he thought of his wife, and feared that she might already have suffocated somewhere in the Melody Lounge.

But Mildred Jeffers was not dead. At that moment she was experiencing the worst terror of her life. Surrounded by acrid smoke, she was crawling along an unknown area in the dark.

"There's no way out!" she heard someone cry.

All at once the fear and the fire and the darkness caught up with her, and she could no longer think clearly or relate herself to the frightening scene. Still on hands and knees she began to crawl in aimless panic, remembering nothing from one second to the next.

When her sense of self returned, she was looking toward a window. Two men were standing in front of it. She ran forward, and they pulled her up on to a radiator on which they stood.

"You'll have to jump!" one of them said.

Mildred had no idea where she was relative to the level of the Melody Lounge, or to the ground outside or the ceiling above her.

Jump? Did he mean up? Down? Outward? Completely disoriented and paralysed by fear, Mildred froze on the window ledge.

"Jump!"

She held back for another moment. Then she pushed herself through toward something, anything, away from the dreadful smoke and fire behind her.

She fell about eight feet. When she struck the ground at the rear of the Grove, she cut her knee slightly. But she was outside and safe. She began to search through the gathering crowd, fervently hoping that Donald had also found a way out of the Melody Lounge.

All was quiet in the Melody Lounge now. Behind the bar, Daniel Weiss, still sitting on the floor and breathing through the wet cloth, became aware that the smoke above him was not as thick and acrid as it had been, and decided that it might be safe to get up. He soaked his cloth once more, placed it over his face, and groped toward the kitchen door. The Lounge was hot and smoky, but he saw no sign of flames. Several times he stumbled over bodies on the floor.

As he entered the kitchen he met a party of terrified women. "You're going the wrong way," Weiss said. "Follow me. I'll take you out the service door."

He guided them across the dark kitchen and through two swinging doors that led to the furnace room. They had reached the base of a stairway leading to the service door when one of the women cried out hysterically:

"He's lost! He's leading us back to the fire!"

Before Weiss could stop them, the women turned and fled. He tried to follow, but could not locate them anywhere.

In spite of their panic, and the pandemonium he could hear upstairs, Weiss somehow remained unruffled. He decided to explore the stairway leading up to the Dining Room. After a few steps, however, he felt heat coming down, and saw bodies slumped on the steps above.

Weiss descended and made another complete circuit of the kitchen, hoping to find the frightened women. When he could not, he made his way back to the service door, where he decided he might as well go out.

He escaped with no more than a slightly sore throat.

In the crowd Weiss joined on Shawmut Street, Stanley Tomaszewski, the bus boy, watched in amazement as the Cocoanut Grove blazed from end to end. Only a few moments before, Stanley had finally found a way of escape for the Melody Lounge patrons he had led into the kitchen. One by one he had helped them wriggle through a small window above a kitchen counter. Though he had been terrified, Stanley had waited until all of the women in the group got through before climbing out himself. As he watched the flames now pouring from the building, he became conscious for the first time of the burns on his hands and forehead.

Another bus boy, still inside the club, was at that moment near hysteria. Tony Marra had reached the kitchen safely after jumping from the spotlight loft. He had run to an exhaust fan, where he stood breathing the smoke-free air until the power failed and the fan stopped. As he began to retch on the smoke, Tony thought he was going to smother.

He turned and ran across the kitchen in response to a sudden notion: the ice cream freezer! He passed through the swinging door that separated the kitchen from the storage room and groped along the wall until he found the freezer. He pulled off one of the round covers and bent over the open hole. Even in the dark he could tell that the flavour it contained was chocolate. The drum was full to the top; there was no room for his head to go in. Tony pulled a second cover—vanilla. But it was full, too.

Tony tried a third—maple-walnut—and found the drum nearly empty. This time he pushed his entire head down into the opening. He felt the ice cream stick to his face and hair, but the air he was breathing was cold and free of smoke. He stayed there, inhaling gratefully, in the maple-walnut drum, until he felt all of the choking sensation ease out of his throat.

Suddenly he heard a familiar sound behind him; it was the heavy thud of one of the meat chest doors. Tony became furious with himself for not having thought of them sooner. There were two such chests in the kitchen; one was the single-door refrigerator in which Donald Jeffers waited. The other was a huge electric chest with three doors. Tony ran across the room to the larger one and groped along the wall until he touched the big metal handle of the nearest door. The smoke began to choke him again. He pulled, and heard the latch click, but he could not open the door. Inside he could hear voices.

"Let me in!" he shouted. "Please let me in! I'm only fifteen years old! Open the door."

The door swung open slightly. Tony shoved his shoulder into the narrow space between it and the wall of the chest. But a big hand was suddenly pressed over his face and he was pushed back.

"Get out of here, kid!" he heard a man say. "It's full. There's no room left."

The big door clicked shut. Tony was left standing there, coughing and crying in the darkness.

He began to run. Tears flowed from his eyes, but he could not hear his own sobs in the din of adults around him. "I can't die here!" he wailed. "I can't die! I've got to get out!"

He passed through a door into a corridor. Not more than twelve feet from him was the exit that John Bradley, the head bartender, had used to take some of the patrons out. But Tony did not even know that it existed, and could not see in the dark. He turned and ran back into the kitchen.

Suddenly he saw light—a window. Tony scrambled up on a counter and wriggled under two hot pipes which partially blocked the window. He smashed the glass and the wooden frame with his foot. Then he crawled through, and felt the welcome sting of cold air on his face.

Tony found himself in an alley which ended on Church Street, behind the night club. As he ran away from the burning building, he rubbed his hands through his sticky hair and licked the ice cream from his fingers.

7

FIRE Alarm Headquarters received the call from Dennis Sullivan's wife at 10.20. More than two minutes was required to ascertain that the earlier call on Box 1514 had been for a different fire. At 10.23 Chief Crowley's third alarm began to sound. Then another citizen phoned to report that flames were shooting out the Piedmont Street doorway of the Grove. At 10.24 Chief Crowley rang a fourth alarm.

The Fire Department had undoubtedly gained a time advantage by virtue of being at the scene with their equipmen ready. But because of the swiftness of the Grove fire, much of this advantage was lost. By the time the men turned their attention to the club, it was afire from the Melody Lounge all the way out to Broadway.

The first firemen to reach the Grove were astonished by a sight they saw on a second floor window ledge. A beautiful girl, wrapped in a fur coat, was sitting there with her lovely legs dangling. She was Dorothy Christie, a Cocoanut Grove show girl, one of the two girls who had not followed Jackie Maver out the Shawmut Street service door.

Under her fur coat Dottie wore an elaborate show-girl costume. Its function was simply to emphasize the beauty of her body. Sitting there on the ledge, Dottie lost none of the poise and grace for which she had been hired. By merely placing herself on display, she instantly caught the firemen's attention, and the first of the ladders went up to her. A fireman climbed it to help her, and Dottie negotiated the descent with perfect dignity.

The only girl still inside the dressing room was Claudia Boyle, from the chorus. She had decided that, fire or not, she wasn't going out into the cold wearing only her skimpy costume. When the others started down the stairs, she zipped open her costume and pulled it off. Stark naked, she began gathering her clothes. Just then the bulbs over the dressing room mirrors went out. A feeble light shone in from the street, but it was not enough to enable her to locate a dress. Claudia groped around until she found her fur coat. She decided it would have to do.

She went to the window beside the one Dorothy Christie had used. She opened it and shouted down. Her cry was heard by a waiter, John Rizzo, who had just escaped from the Dining Room. Rizzo saw Claudia poised as though about to jump.

"Wait! Claudia! Wait a second!" He ran to a spot directly beneath the window and braced himself. Claudia leaped. The coat billowed up like a parachute as she tensed herself for the landing. She hit Rizzo squarely, and they both tumbled to the sidewalk. Then Claudia bounced to her feet, bundled the coat around her, and—unhurt—moved away from the building.

At about the same time, another girl—injured, terrified, and heartbroken—crawled forward on the Shawmut Street sidewalk and lay there, her hands clasped together inside a leopardskin muff.

Her name was Joyce Spector, and she had escaped from

the Melody Lounge by a tortuous route. At the first hint of fire in the basement room, Joyce had left her fiancé and gone upstairs to get her new $800 leopardskin coat from the cloakroom. The matching muff she had kept with her, for it contained her make-up. On her way to the cloakroom, Joyce paused long enough to alert two women in the powder room that a fire had started downstairs and they had better hurry out.

In that brief interval she lost her advantage over the crowd coming up from the Melody Lounge. She was bowled forward past the revolving door and pushed into the Dining Room, where she was knocked under a table just as the lights went out. Joyce slowly made her way across to the Shawmut Street door on her hands and knees. Several times she hid under tables for protection against the crowd. It was a frightening ordeal, and she was never certain that she would survive.

Now she lay near the gutter at the edge of the sidewalk, unable to find the strength to rise. Her face and hair were burned and her body bruised, but she felt little pain—the cold air had already begun to numb her.

Behind Joyce, a frightened line of patrons streamed out of the door. Many of them fell on the sidewalk and into the gutter. She could tell by the grotesque manner in which they lay that most of them were dead. Among them was a short, middle-aged man who had been sitting beside her in the Lounge. She and her fiancé had overheard enough of his conversation to learn that he and his wife were celebrating their twenty-fifth wedding anniversary. Joyce had noted at the time that neither the man nor his wife looked like the sort of people who went to the Cocoanut Grove often, if at all.

Now he lay dead on the sidewalk, his body disfigured by

burns. Joyce concluded that his wife had probably fallen and died somewhere inside the club. She pushed her hands tighter into the leopardskin muff and prayed that her fiancé, Justin Morgan, had had better fortune than they.

While Joyce Spector lay on the Shawmut Street sidewalk, a Gloucester sailor named Stanley Viator was performing one of the most heroic acts of the night.

Viator had just happened to be passing through the area when the fire broke out. When he saw that many were still trapped inside, he dashed into the club through the open Shawmut Street door. A moment later he reappeared, leading two men. When they were safely out, he ran back inside. Three times he did this, each time returning with patrons whom he guided to safety. The fourth time, he did not come out.

A Coast Guardsman, Clifford Johnson, was then attempting similar rescues at the Broadway door. Johnson was a farm boy from Sumner, Missouri, and that night was dating a Winthrop girl, Estelle Balkan, for the first time. He had met her that afternoon through a friend. In his effort to get her safely out of the New Cocoanut Grove Lounge, Clifford had held her hand and tried to pull her through the door after him. But at the last moment he had lost her, and had been thrust on to the sidewalk alone.

Now he dashed repeatedly through the flames raging inside the door. The vestibule was blocked by screaming victims, some of whom he dragged to safety. Clifford was seen to go back into the burning Lounge four times. On his last attempt he was halted by a pile of bodies which had accumulated in the entry. He had no alternative but to give up his search for Estelle and get out.

When he emerged he was enveloped in flames. As he hit the sidewalk its rough surface rasped and scraped his burned flesh. The rush of pain was so intense that he fainted instantly. He lay there blackened, almost naked, with more than half his skin burned away. But he was alive, and even though he was unconscious, he was clinging to life tenaciously.

Around the corner from where Clifford fell, Police Captain Buccigross and a patrolman who had just arrived ran across the Grove parking lot. Buccigross had escaped from the Broadway exit shortly before Clifford Johnson began his rescues there. Now he was intent upon a rescue of his own.

He could see, on the flat roof of the main building, nearly a dozen employees, apparently entertainers and musicians. They were running back and forth along the parapet, looking for a place to jump. Below, a parking lot attendant was gazing up at them helplessly.

"We've got to get them down!" Buccigross exclaimed. "Pull out some of the seat cushions from those cars and bring them over here!"

The three men laid a square of four cushions on the ground near the building. One by one, the men trapped on the roof leaped at the target. The moment they landed, the trio on the ground caught them and prevented them from bouncing. Incredibly, nobody was hurt.

Buccigross then hurried across the lot to Broadway, where the patrolman's car was parked. He slid behind the wheel and snatched the microphone from the dashboard. "This is Captain Buccigross," he told the dispatcher. "I just came out of the Cocoanut Grove—there are bodies everywhere! Get the Commissioner—and send all the help you can spare!"

While Buccigross called Headquarters, a breathless reporter rushed past the police car toward the New Lounge door, where he was knocked to the ground by a sudden exodus of patrons. He was Nat Kline, the *Globe* reporter who had been keeping the log in the press room at Police Headquarters, a half mile away.

When the second alarm was skipped, Nat and the other reporters had phoned their city editors. After hanging up, Nat ran all the way to the Grove without stopping or slowing down. He was the first reporter on the scene.

When Nat was knocked to the ground, he landed in a sitting position facing the Broadway door. A steady stream of victims filed past him—men and women whose eyes bulged and whose faces were contorted with pain. They staggered woodenly. Dolls . . . they looked to Nat precisely like wooden dolls.

As Nat watched in amazement, most of those coming out collapsed on the pavement.

Firemen scurried around Kline, lifting victims and placing them in a row along the sidewalk, clearing a path for those still coming out.

Kline glanced down the block and saw a sign, "Mario's Restaurant," at the far end of Shawmut Street. He hurried toward it, fishing in his pocket for a nickel. He had to zig-zag around patrons who were staggering out of the Shawmut Street door in the same wooden manner as the others.

Nat ran into Mario's, found a phone booth, and dialled rapidly. The *Globe* operator flipped his call on to the board and made him wait.

"Dolls!" Nat muttered to himself. "Little wooden dolls!"

When the operator rang the city desk, Phil Denvir, the city editor, snatched up the phone. "City room!" he snapped.

"Phil! My God, Phil!" said Kline. "They're laying them on the sidewalk!" Then he slammed the receiver on to its hook and raced back to the fire.

Eddie Roth, who arrived a moment later, made just as

cryptic a call to the Boston *Herald*. "My God! They're all dead!" he said. That was all.

Dick Folsom's call to the Boston *Post* was answered by Herb Kenny. "I'm at the Cocoanut Grove!" Folsom said. "It's terrible! Terrible!"

The city editors, accustomed to their reporters' usual tone of bored detachment, deduced as much from these messages as if they had contained specific detail. They began marshalling their forces for coverage of the biggest news story ever to occur in Boston.

The mayor of Boston, Maurice Tobin, and his fire commissioner, William Arthur Reilly, arrived at the fire at 10.29. They had been dining at the Parker House, a mile or so downtown, with a few of the coaches and players from the defeated Boston College team.

When the mayor appeared on the scene, fire companies which had responded to the third and fourth alarms were attaching hoses, raising ladders, and making rescues at the doorways. The fire was now too dangerous to permit entrance through any of the Grove's openings except the Shawmut Street service door. But there, two firemen made their way through the smoke and disappeared up the stairs. They were Frank Marr and Charlie Johnson, both assigned to the rescue unit.

Marr and Johnson made a futile search of the rooms above the New Lounge, then ran down two flights of stairs to the basement. Marr swept his flashlight back and forth in an effort to locate victims, most of whom lay coughing and retching on the floor. One of the first to jump up and run toward him was Billy Payne, who had directed patrons toward the refrigerators and now feared they might be smothering inside.

Johnson rushed over to the larger of the two walk-in refrigerators. He opened all three doors and called for those inside to form a line. He held his flashlight on them while they joined hands, then led them across the smoke-filled basement and up the stairway to the Shawmut Street service door. Then he returned to the smaller refrigerator and freed Donald Jeffers, the two terrified women, and the waiter.

Marr and Johnson were soon joined by other firemen who helped them search the basement and round up remaining victims. Marr then reported to Lieutenant Myles Murphy, on Shawmut Street, that he could find no one else alive downstairs.

Lieutenant Murphy had just ordered his men to break the plate glass windows that lined the entire side of the main building on Shawmut Street. As the firemen shattered the glass, they discovered a flimsy wall behind it. They were able to pry out huge sections of this wall providing wide exits for the dwindling stream of patrons who were waiting to pass through the double door.

When Safety Director Walsh, still helping the few now arriving at the double door, saw that they could flee easily through the open wall, he left his post and ran to the phone booth in Mario's restaurant. He called Civil Defence Headquarters, which, because of the war, kept personnel on duty twenty-four hours a day.

"This is John Walsh," he said. "There's a very bad fire in the Cocoanut Grove. I want a full alert. Everything! This is a disaster!"

8

AN incredible set of circumstances, that evening at the Cocoanut Grove, had put men trained to respond to any emergency at the scene when the emergency arose. But even the skill of the firemen, the safety director, and the police captain was no match for the speed of the flames nor the magnitude of the disaster.

Fire apparatus from every section of the city was now scattered around the block on which the Cocoanut Grove stood. The streets were cluttered with all manner of equipment—pumping engines, ladder trucks, hose wagons, rescue units, lighting plants, chiefs' cars—even a van equipped with a public address system. Firemen were scurrying everywhere, carrying axes, hoses, stretchers, and lights.

By 10.35 the Fire Department was waging a well-co-ordinated attack on the blaze.

Lieutenant Murphy, satisfied with the Shawmut Street evacuation from the Dining Room, ran back to the Broadway door from which brilliant orange flames spewed far out over the street. Murphy ducked under the blaze and charged into the vestibule. Three other firemen followed. But they were blocked by the same barrier that had halted Clifford

Johnson a few minutes before—dead victims heaped in the entry. Beyond the gruesome wall could be heard the cries of those trapped within.

By gestures, Murphy told two of the firemen to begin pulling out bodies, while he and the third man would try to get inside. He snapped his mask into position and crawled over the heap.

Although the heat was fierce, Murphy and his partner managed to wriggle into the Lounge. To the left of the inner door was a corner formed by the Broadway wall and the entry partition. Because the flames were being drawn through the entry, the corner was comparatively fire-free. The two men ducked into the corner, and turned to face the blaze. Murphy saw a woman's foot and made a grab for it but was driven back by the flames. Despite his mask the hot gas seared his throat as he breathed. He retreated again. It was hopeless, he decided, to attempt further rescues until something was done to quench the fire.

Just then he heard the blows of axes. The men outside were trying to smash two tall glass-brick windows in the Broadway wall. The glass was thick and smooth; many of the blows just glanced off. At last Murphy saw the men outside knock out a piece near the sill. After pushing it into the Lounge, they were able to insert wrecking bars to pry out other bricks. Murphy pulled off his mask and shouted, "Give us a line, quick! We can't live in here!"

A nozzle was pushed through the opening. "Hit the ceiling with it!" Murphy cried. "We've got live victims here!"

The hosemen pulled back on the nozzle valve and a powerful stream of water shot up, bouncing a spray over the front part of the Lounge. Huge clouds of steam rose around Murphy and his partner as they tried again to advance into the flames. But still they could not go far enough to reach victims.

"Give us another line!" Murphy hollered over the roar of the water. "It's wicked in here!"

A hole was broken in the adjacent glass-brick window. When a second hose was turned on, Murphy and his partner were able to advance to the area near the inner door. They began hauling bodies from the pile there, passing them to the men in the vestibule, where a third water line had been put into play. But even though Murphy stood directly beneath the double spray deflected from the ceiling, his hands were burned by the heat of the bodies. Each time flame from the back of the Lounge shot forward, he had to retreat. Doggedly he advanced into the blaze again and again. He and his partner heaved out thirty bodies before the inner doorway was cleared.

Around the block, on Piedmont Street, Deputy Chief John McDonough and his men were battling equally ferocious flames. Fire was still spurting out of the Foyer in a trajectory almost parallel to the ground. Suddenly McDonough saw, crammed in the doorway, what appeared to be a statue. He lunged under the flames to remove it, and felt the shape and resilience of a human being. It seemed incredible to him that he could have mistaken the form for a statue. Then he looked again and saw more stiff figures just like it inside.

McDonough and his men continued to dive under the blaze and reach blindly for bodies. They would grasp an arm or a pair of legs and pull backward until they could safely lift the victims and carry them out. Hosemen gave them protection by shooting streams just above the rescuers' heads. An ugly pile of bodies quickly accumulated on the sidewalk.

McDonough was on his way back from depositing a body when he heard a tinkling sound above him. Broken glass began to shower down on him and his crew. He saw that it fell from the marquee, whose metal now glowed a dull red from the heat of the fire. Before the blaze struck it, the glass had been neat white lettering that spelled out "Cocoanut Grove."

Thirty feet to the left of the doorway where McDonough's men worked, four firemen heaved on wrecking bars inserted in the jamb of the fire door at the top of the Melody Lounge stairs. This was the door designed to be opened by a single flip of the panic bar. The firemen had to break off part of the lock before the door would budge.

Inside was a pile of charred bodies—four, five, and six deep—packed from one wall of the passageway to the other. The bodies had to be separated and carried out before firemen could enter that end of the Foyer.

Although most of the bodies were now out of the circle where the revolving door had been, the fire still prevented entry. Two firemen who tried to dash through got close enough to see agonized victims actually being consumed by flames. The men tried another rush, but it was impossible; the Foyer was now a furnace. There was no choice but to pour water through the doorway no matter who was hurt or barred from escape, in order to diminish the blaze so that rescuers could enter.

Finally the water streams quelled the fierceness of flames in the doorway. But the first rescuers could not immediately reach the living victims they heard still crying for help. Another gruesome wall of dead just inside the Foyer had to be removed first.

While these dead were being carried out, the commander of the Fire Department, Chief Samuel Pope, arrived on Piedmont Street. Pope had sped to the scene from a Back Bay hotel, where he and his wife had been dining. Before he had a chance to confer with his subordinates, Chief Pope's arm was seized by the building commissioner, James Mooney, who had also just arrived.

"Chief! I know where the control panel is for the rolling roof!" Mooney said. "If we can get it open, it may draw some of the fire out!"

Mooney and Pope hurried around the block to the Shawmut Street service door, where firemen were running in and out through the smoke. Mooney led Pope through the backstage passageway, which was now clear of patrons, to a steel electrical control box located at the base of the stairs. Mooney tried to open the steel door, but it was too hot to touch. Pope ordered a nearby fireman to pry it open, and Mooney then gingerly flipped the proper switches. But by then all power in the building was dead, and the roof would not roll back.

Pope led Mooney out, then ran back to the Piedmont Street side to direct operations there.

He ordered his men to break panes, sashes, and casements out of four big windows so that water could be shot into the building without blocking the entry of rescuers. But no sooner were the windows cleared than the unburned gases exploded out of them, and the fire fighters were forced back. Some of the victims inside tried to escape through these windows, but few succeeded. The heat was so intense that they would blister, blacken, and fall before they reached safety. The few who made it to the sidewalk were hideously burned.

In an effort to draw off some of this flame, firemen began chopping holes in the roof. Each break-through was followed by a furious rush of smoke and fire as the trapped gases burst into the open air.

More hose lines were connected and water poured into

the building, but the fire subsided only slightly. The blue satin, the rattan, and the fiercely burning leatherette inside the club were producing new volumes of flames every second.

Out on Broadway, the men with axes and pinch bars kept hacking away at the remaining glass bricks. In spite of several hose lines now pouring hundreds of gallons of water into the New Lounge, the volume of fire there was prodigious.

Although repeatedly stalled by the belching fire, the men at the windows kept working in close, chopping and prying whenever they could.

Suddenly they heard a frantic scream from inside. The head, shoulders, and trunk of a man came through one of the holes. Two of the firemen reached up to hold him away from the broken glass. But he was off balance and fell forward, impaling himself on its jagged edges. The firefighters had to turn their faces away when they saw his blood bubble on contact with the hot glass.

The one place in the Grove where the fire burned as fires are expected to burn was in the passageway between the Dining Room and the New Lounge. The blaze in this passageway was fed by oxygen from the broken windows and doors. Flames licked and clung around the two-by-fours and corner beams, burning with a crackling sound and billowing grey smoke. This was residual fire, and the only way to put it out was to soak down every inch of every beam.

Gradually the firemen began to win control over the blaze. Soon they were able to drag several hose lines into the club and work at close quarters.

The men who went inside, however, noticed a sudden change in the sounds they had been hearing. The cries of hysteria and panic were gone, replaced by occasional moans and whimpers. During the next minute or so, even these faint sounds died out.

Those who were still alive inside could now do no more for themselves. They lay unconscious, burned, and concealed among the dead and the debris.

The time was 10.45. Less than half an hour had passed since the first fire company switched its attention from the grey saloon car parked at Stuart and Carver.

The firemen had done all that could be expected of them, and more. They had braved heat and flame worse than any of them had ever experienced.

Police, waiters, passers-by—everyone had done his best.

But even this was far from enough.

9

A DARK-ROBED figure stood in the Grove's smouldering Foyer and wept without shame at the death and agony he saw everywhere. Father Damian Sano, O.F.M., a Fire Department chaplain who had arrived with the third alarm companies, had a heartbreaking duty to perform.

For several minutes Father Sano had been forced to wait on Piedmont Street, watching fire so violent that it blackened and cracked the stucco on the archway at the Grove's main entrance. When the first firemen had succeeded in passing under the archway, he tried to follow, but Chief McDonough held him back. The chief insisted that Father Sano stay out of the building until the fire in the Foyer was extinguished and the bodies in the doorway were removed.

As each victim was retrieved, Father Sano knelt on the sidewalk to administer the last rites of the Roman Catholic Church. When the doorway was finally cleared and the firemen were able to move into the building under the protection of a water curtain, Father Sano followed. Now he stood in the steaming Foyer; victims of the catastrophe were everywhere on the floor around him.

His obligation as a priest was clear. Unable to determine the faith of victims, or whether they were alive or dead, he must give conditional absolution to all. One by one he approached each body and pressed his fingers to its forehead. "*Si vives*," he began, "If you are alive . . ." Then "*Si tu es capax, ego te absolvo*." "If you are capable, I absolve you . . ."

The air was stifling. The priest's eyes ran with tears, partly from the smoke but primarily from grief. After ministering to the first four or five victims, his anointing fingers were raw and swollen from burns received when he touched the hot flesh. Twice Father Sano tripped over bodies as he tried to hurry along beside moving stretchers so as not to impede the rescuers.

He saw a fireman accidentally kick the body of a woman; the form reacted with a spasm. "She's alive!" he cried. "Maybe she has a chance!"

He helped the stretcher bearers lift the woman from the debris. God help this poor creature if she were to survive, he thought, for her face, neck, and shoulders were blistered and blackened.

As Father Sano continued his ministrations in the Foyer, the air became clearer and cooler. Portable lights were brought in; their bright beams only emphasized to him the enormity of the disaster. Before the Foyer was evacuated he gave conditional absolution to nearly two hundred victims.

By this time volunteers—mostly servicemen—were helping the firemen. A Coast Guardsman and a taxi driver named Henry Watson carried an empty litter toward the Shawmut Street side of the club, and made their way to the Terrace. There, Watson spotted a body whose feet wore a pair of beautifully tooled leather cowboy boots.

"Here he is!" Watson exclaimed. "Is he dead?"

The Coast Guardsman bent close to the body. "He's breathing. But he's hurt bad. My God! How he must have taken it!"

They lifted the tall figure on to their litter and carried him out. At the curb was a police ambulance that already had one victim inside. Watson and the serviceman pushed their litter into the van. A patrolman climbed in, and the ambulance pulled away.

Buck Jones was taking his last ride.

The first fireman to reach the room where the fire started was Frank Marr, who went back through the basement when he learned that firemen on Piedmont Street were blocked by bodies on the Melody Lounge stairway. Marr discovered the concealed door that led from the kitchen into the Lounge. Through the lingering smoke he saw the large oval bar. Incredibly, men and women were sitting on several stools around it.

"Come on, you people! You'll have to get out!" he shouted.

Then it struck him. Those at the bar were either propped against one another or slumped over the bar top. They were all dead.

Marr saw many more bodies at the tables, on the settees, and on the floor. He hurried back to Shawmut Street for men to help him carry the victims out.

Among the dead who were evacuated through the darkened basement were Justin Morgan, Joyce Spector's fiancé; and Harold Goldenberg and Florence Zimmerman, the couple who had sat in the corner with Maurice Levy and his wife. The firemen also found a man who lay not far from the body of a pretty girl; he may have been the cause of the tragedy—the one who had unscrewed the light bulb in the palm tree so that he and his girl could have privacy.

Upstairs other dead were being found and identified. John and Claudia O'Neill, the Cambridge bride and groom, lay together near the centre of the dance floor. The rescuers had no time to consider the possible significance of their proximity; Claudia and John were carried out separately and put into different vehicles. Anna O'Neill, Claudia's sister-in-law and maid of honour, and Johnny Doyle, her husband's best man, were also taken out. All four were dead.

Eleanor Chiampa, the fifteen-year-old girl whose older brother, Benjamin, had given her so exciting a day, was sent to Massachusetts Memorial Hospital, where she died. Benjamin, in fairly good condition, went to Peter Bent Brigham Hospital. But his wife, Jennie, was dead when she was brought out of the club.

Jake Slate, the tobacco dealer, was evacuated through the narrow door toward which he and his wife, Ethel, were headed when the fumes overcame them. Jake was examined on the street and found to be unconscious and burned, but breathing well. He was sent to Massachusetts General Hospital. But Ethel was already dead.

Some of the victims were so badly burned they were unrecognizable. But many of them appeared untouched by fire; it seemed impossible that they were dead. Firemen tried to revive several with oxygen and artificial respiration, but there was no response. The gases they had inhaled had asphyxiated them too long before.

Of those who had fainted after running out of the club, many died immediately. They had breathed carbon monoxide and other poisons during their violent struggles inside, and the shock of cold air had been enough to stop their hearts.

John Walsh, the safety director, knelt over the crouched form of a man wearing a women's white fur coat. The man was hysterical, nearly overcome by smoke, and obviously not in control of his actions. He had just been helped out of the basement. Walsh slapped the man's cheeks and shook his shoulders. "It's all right. You're outside now. Try to pull yourself together."

Mickey Alpert, the bandleader, looked around anxiously, then buried his face in his hands.

Nearby, Captain Buccigross spotted the superintendent of the Police Department, Edward Fallon, and went over to report what he had done so far. But before Buccigross could begin, Fallon said sharply, "Captain, go to your station and get into proper uniform."

Astonished by the command, Buccigross protested, "But Eddie . . . I . . ."

"That's an order!" Fallon snapped.

Buccigross turned away, and Fallon joined the cluster of city officials conferring in the parking lot.

The mayor, the commissioners of the Fire, Police, and Building departments, the fire chief, and the safety director discussed their most acute problem: evacuation. Dead, dying, and gravely injured victims were piled up everywhere. Broadway was a one-way street, only three lanes wide. Shawmut and Piedmont Streets, both very narrow, were also one-way. A route had to be worked out for ambulances to approach the club on the narrow streets, pick up victims, and drive away quickly.

To compound the problem, there was a woeful shortage of transportation. Vehicles would have to be commandeered, it was decided, to carry the injured to hospitals.

The police began seizing anything that had wheels and power. Taxis, newspaper trucks, and private cars were loaded and sent to Boston City Hospital or the Southern Mortuary.

The rows of bodies along the sidewalks now extended from the Shawmut and Piedmont doorways all the way out to Broadway, causing rescuers to walk too far to do their grisly job efficiently. Fallon ordered officers to break open the doors of a garage opposite the Grove's main entrance. The firemen then began piling the bodies on the concrete floor. On Shawmut Street another makeshift morgue was set up in a publishing house.

The scene was dominated by the dying and the dead. Even the emergency morgues could not accommodate the enormous influx of bodies. Corpses soon had to be stacked on top of one another, creating the impression that was to persist in the minds of witnesses:

"They were stacking them like cordwood!"

The simile was brutally accurate; the piles were uniform, many of the bodies black and shapeless. No one in the crowd had ever seen so many dead in one place.

The American Railway Express Company was asked to send every van for which a driver could be found. When the vans arrived they were used exclusively for the dead. Each truck was held until a large load was packed on to it—bodies piled five and six high in several rows. A policeman would mount each running board and the driver would pull away, his grim load swaying weirdly with the motion of the van.

To move the injured, the Park Square area was drained of every available taxi. Motion picture film transfer trucks, garaged in the area, were found to make good ambulances. Even newspaper trucks, in the process of dropping off their downtown deliveries, were commandeered to take survivors away.

At the start of the evacuation, nearly all victims, living

87

and dead, were sent to Boston City Hospital, placing upon it the heaviest casualty burden ever borne by an American medical institution. But the situation at the Grove was far too urgent for rescuers to consider problems developing elsewhere.

Volunteers were assembled from all over the city. The Coast Guard made available three hundred men from its ships and headquarters on the water front. Every military officer in the area was asked to organize enlisted men into litter squads.

Then the Red Cross people began to arrive. The Boston Metropolitan Chapter headquarters had quickly alerted more than one thousand staff members and volunteers. Requests for additional supplies and equipment were already being acted upon in western Massachusetts, New Hampshire, Rhode Island, Connecticut, and New York. The blue-grey clad workers converged on the scene, the hospitals, and Red Cross Centres like so many anxious ants. Thirty-nine Red Cross ambulances reached the Grove, formed a line along Broadway, and began taking away victims. Four mobile canteens, one of them called away from the Opera House where it was about to serve an audience attending *This Is the Army*, drove to the area to provide coffee and refreshments to the weary rescue workers.

On learning of the disaster, Red Cross officials had correctly anticipated what was to be the most urgent need in the crisis: blood, plasma, and intravenous fluids. Blood programme directors all over New England immediately began loading their reserves into automobiles, trains and aeroplanes for Boston.

One Red Cross volunteer was Jim Carter, supervisor of physical education for Quincy schools. He had been in bed when the telephone call came, but his station wagon, registered and equipped as a Red Cross ambulance, was ready for service.

Carter put on long underwear, for the telephone message indicated he would be working outside most of the night. As he passed the bedroom where his own daughter, Betty, slept, he muttered, "Thank God." Betty was an extremely pretty Syracuse University coed. Only a current romance with a boy in New York had prevented her from accepting a date that might have included the Cocoanut Grove.

By 11.00 P.M., when Carter reached the Grove, the rescuers were working with brisk efficiency. The supplies were taken from his car, but he was told it would not be necessary for him to drive. He made a circuit of the building and decided his most useful job would be to assist the priests, ministers, and rabbis now working with Father Sano.

Carter helped the clergymen turn and move victims so that rites could be performed and faint requests heard. He was aghast at the appearance of the dead—the cordwood analogy struck him immediately. Then he examined one man whose only affliction seemed to be minor burns on the tips of his fingers; the man had been placed with the dead.

Carter suggested to a Red Cross official that some of these unburned victims might respond to artificial respiration.

"We've tried it," he was told. "Look at their colour. That cherry red—it means carbon monoxide poisoning. Nothing can help them now."

Carter watched the young servicemen working quietly and swiftly among the dead. He thought he was immune to the shock of seeing distorted human bodies, yet he found himself on the verge of nausea several times. But the servicemen, most of them mere kids of eighteen or nineteen, did their job without flinching. Carter experienced a sudden feeling of confidence in the outcome of the war, with boys such as these available.

Carter watched the well-organized pattern of evacuation. Empty vehicles moved down Piedmont and Shawmut Streets toward Broadway and stopped at the doorways, where they were loaded. To each vehicle carrying live victims someone was assigned to give first aid during the ride to the hospital.

Briefing some of these riders was a South Boston nurse, whose coat and uniform were now badly soiled from contact with victims she had been treating. Called by her hospital to work in the emergency, she had taken a taxi, but was halted at a police line several blocks from the Grove. A police officer explained that there was little hope the cab could get through, so she got out and walked to the Grove. There she spent the night giving first aid. Though she had several opportunities to ride in ambulances going to her hospital, she decided she could be far more useful where she was. Many of the injured were so near death that only swift, expert treatment could enable them to survive the ambulance ride.

One of the ambulance riders instructed by the nurse was Nina Underwood, a twenty-year-old Red Cross aide. Nina made fifteen trips to hospitals. Nine of the victims she rode with were D.O.A.—dead on arrival. Six of these died during the screaming ride, after Nina had done everything she could to keep them alive.

The block around the Grove was teeming with spectators. As entertainment in the nearby theatres ended, many from their audiences gathered to watch the grim activities. Congestion became so serious that police began ordering people away, threatening arrest if they refused to go. But the crowds would not disperse, for the horror gripped them in morbid fascination. They kept shuffling closer, hypnotized by the sight of bodies being carried out of the Grove.

The police superintendent had to assign twenty men, sorely needed for other tasks, to patrol the Grove block, forcing spectators back so that rescuers would have room to work.

Superintendent Fallon sent another group of officers to close the twenty or so taverns in the area, even though it was nearly an hour before the Saturday night curfew. Civilian patrons were told to go home. Men in uniform were ordered to report to an officer of their service in charge at the Grove.

It had grown colder. The temperature had dropped to twenty-eight degrees. The spray of the fire hoses and the leakage of water from the building froze on the apparatus, the streets, and the sidewalks. Litter bearers had to creep cautiously from the Grove's doors until they reached ground where they could get a footing.

The crowd was subdued and silent, except for the weeping sounds of relatives and lovers who waited, hopeful that the next to come out, perhaps not badly hurt, would be the one they sought.

But as the cold minutes passed, fewer and fewer victims were brought out of the Grove alive. More and more of the vehicles were sent directly to the morgues. The mute presence of death widened through the area until it dominated everything.

10

THE Cocoanut Grove fire was a disaster—and a disaster is news.

At 11.05, when Chief Pope sounded a fifth alarm, newspapermen rushed to telephones at several places near the scene. They called their papers to report that, although the fire was extinguished, Chief Pope needed more men and equipment to speed the evacuation.

The Boston *Globe*'s response to this message was typical of what occurred in the four other city rooms.

Phil Denvir, thirty-six-year-old city editor at the *Globe*, received the message from Paul Plakias, a reporter he had sent from the office to join Nat Kline at the fire. Denvir hung up and turned to Bob Carr, an office boy, who was telephoning off-duty members of the editorial staff. "If they're not home, find out where they are," Denvir said. "I don't care what they're doing, tell them to get in here!"

Denvir, who could be as canny as a field marshal when deploying men on a fast-breaking event, knew he was handling the biggest local story in the *Globe*'s history. He was also keenly aware of the opposition. For, in 1942, Boston was a highly competitive newspaper city. The *Globe* published three morning editions and four in the afternoon. The

Hearst organization circulated the *Daily Record* from early in the evening until morning, then continued with the Boston *American*. The Boston *Herald*, a morning paper, was followed by its evening companion, the Boston *Traveler*. The big morning newspaper was the Boston *Post*, widely circulated all over New England. Though the *Christian Science Monitor* was regarded as an international publication that did not compete with the others for local news, its editors also wanted all possible information on the fire.

All of the papers had been alerted by the alarm at 10.23. They had immediately sent reporters and photographers to the Grove.

After Denvir had sent Nat Kline from Police Headquarters, he called for a photographer from the *Globe*'s photographers' loft. The cameraman, Edison Farrand, happened to be holding a pretty good poker hand at the time. He dropped the cards and headed for the Grove in a taxi.

It was less than five minutes later that Kline, breathless from his long run to the fire, put in the excited call from Mario's Restaurant. When Denvir heard Kline say, "They're laying them on the sidewalk," he pulled out all the stops. He called for a second photographer, and it was then that he sent Plakias and a third reporter to the Grove. Two other newsmen he ordered to cover City and Massachusetts General hospitals. As an afterthought, he sent office boys to help the reporters at the scene.

Not until all these men had left the office did Denvir realize he had virtually "emptied the barn." There was no one in sight capable of handling the rewrite on such a monumental story.

But Denvir recovered quickly. He discovered that one of his best rewrite men, Sam Cutler, was playing cribbage in the sports department. Denvir told Cutler to begin organizing a story for the upcoming edition. He told an office boy to begin telephoning correspondents, and to hold each on the line for assignment, to go either to the fire or to the homes of victims to get "handout" pictures.

Each time a reporter phoned from the Grove, Denvir quizzed him on latest developments, then turned the call over to Cutler. By the time Plakias called to report the fifth alarm, Cutler had put together a sketchy story which he had sent along, a page at a time, to be set in type.

Plakias was now in charge of *Globe* men at the scene, for Kline had returned to the office to describe the fire to an artist making a sketch to show the night club's interior. Although Plakias was abreast of developments at the fire, he had been delayed on arrival by the necessity of checking an outrageous rumour.

The story concerned the body of a pretty young girl found in a telephone booth just inside the Foyer. Untouched by fire, she had died of asphyxiation. The discovery of her body made a strong impression on everyone who heard of it.

"They found a girl in the phone booth!" The word had spread quickly through the crowd.

She had been murdered. Plakias was told. She had been strangled and hidden in the phone booth, and her killer had set the fire to conceal his crime.

The story was preposterous, but Plakias could not discount it entirely until he learned that the fire had started accidentally in the palm tree downstairs.

Another story that reporters heard early after their arrival was of the escape of the baby, Richard Tracy, from the apartment above the New Lounge. But what a yarn it had become by then!

The baby, so the story went, was the child of one of the chorus girls to whom it had been born out of wedlock. The young mother had put the child to sleep in an old wardrobe trunk and left him in the care of a kindly handyman while she went down to dance before the patrons. Pure soap opera, it seemed fantastic that such a tale could be repeated in the midst of so terrible a disaster.

While Plakias was seeking accurate information, a resourceful *Globe* cameraman, Bill Ennis, was taking flash pictures at several points around the Grove. He was assisted by four soldiers, each of them an expert photographer, but none of them equipped with a camera.

The four were former *Globe* photographers, now stationed in Boston, who had visited the *Globe* to play poker with their old friends. When the call came for Ennis to go to the fire, they decided to accompany him. The cab bearing the five arrived at Piedmont Street. Ennis and three of the soldiers got out. In the brief interval it took for the fourth, Harry Holbrook, to pay the fare, the first of his buddies had been handed the body of a girl. He passed it to the second, who passed it to the third. Holbrook was given the body after he had taken only a few steps from the cab door. He put the girl in the taxi and told the driver to take her to City Hospital.

The incident alerted the five men to the scope of the disaster. They went to work immediately, the soldiers lining up picture possibilities for Ennis. Each told him the focus distance and best angle. Ennis made the flash exposure, then ran on to the next.

After he had exposed six plates, one of Ennis' friends located a cab to rush the pictures back to the *Globe*.

One of these early pictures, showing bodies lying on the cobbled street, was wired across the country by the Associated Press. By a fluke of edition times, it was published in Los Angeles before it hit the street in Boston.

The fire was a difficult story to cover. All of the news-papers had early editions on Saturday nights, so scraps of detail had to be telephoned in as soon as they were learned in order to meet deadlines. No one at the Grove, however, seemed to possess reliable information. It was impossible for reporters to learn whether twenty victims had been taken away, or one hundred, or perhaps more.

Many in the crowd had escaped from the fire, but they were too wrought up by their own terror—or too concerned with finding lost ones—to talk to reporters.

Two such escapees, Pepper Russell and Connie Warren, shivered in their skimpy chorus costumes and wept audibly as they made their way through the crowd. Pepper was look-ing for Al Willette, the saxophone player who had col-lapsed near the stage after the struggle with the bass drum. Connie was searching for her husband, a cashier in the club, unaware that he had died in a desperate rush across the Dining Room to save her.

When she first saw the bodies being carried out of the Grove, Connie sobbed uncontrollably, convinced that her husband hadn't had a chance. As Pepper tried to console Connie, a photographer took their picture. Both were too cold, sad, and sick to protest.

Pepper put her arm around Connie and tried to persuade her that there was still reason to hope the men would be all right. Both men knew the club, she said, and she and Connie had already seen that other employees had escaped without injury. "Let's go around one more time," Pepper suggested. "They're probably looking for us." But, as they moved slowly past spectators and rescuers, Pepper realized that she had convinced herself no more than Connie that their men were safe.

Because of their conspicuous costumes, the girls were con-

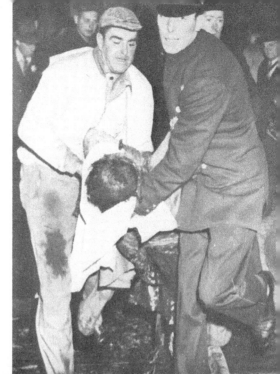

In addition to servicemen, fire fighters, and police, volunteers from nearby areas assisted in evacuating victims from the club. Below, *Globe* photographer Harry Holbrook, then a serviceman, carries the body of a girl to the cab that he and other *Globe* photographers had taken to the fire. (*Photos by William Ennis*)

So desperate was the evacuation problem that numerous volunteers, including patrons who had just escaped from the burning club, helped carry victims to safety. These two photographs were among the first taken by William Ennis as he raced from one spot to another after arriving at the fire.

fronted by reporters several times as they moved around the Grove. Pepper gave one of them her name when she was asked, but would not consent to an interview. Connie was too overwhelmed even to give her name.

At last the girls were taken by a Red Cross worker to a room in the nearby Hotel Bradford where there were other survivors of the fire. Both of the girls were chilled to the bone. They were given hot coffee and told to lie down on two vacant beds.

Pepper sipped two or three times at her coffee, realizing only then how cold and tired she was. She lay back on the bed. When she closed her eyes they smarted from exposure to the smoke. She felt broken with sadness and fatigue. She lay there hoping that, in spite of the voices of people in the room talking only of death and horror, she would be able to fall asleep.

She had barely begun to relax when, suddenly, she felt every muscle in her body respond to a new sensation of shock.

It was a man's hand on her knee, and moving. She opened her eyes to see him leering at her. The whole impact of the terrible night welled up in her all at once. She screamed and jumped up from the bed, then burst into sobs on the shoulder of a woman nearby.

Two men pounced on the lecher and shoved him out of the room. The woman tried to comfort Pepper, and encouraged her to lie back on the bed under a blanket. But Pepper knew it would be impossible to gain any rest now.

Another woman in the confused crowd from whom reporters tried to get information was Marion Bizzozero. She had been buffeted considerably in her passage through the narrow door at the left of the stage in the Dining Room.

She had injured her leg, and her throat was raw from the smoke she had inhaled, but she saw from the many bodies outside that she had been one of the lucky ones. She hoped her husband had been lucky too.

As Marion made her way through the throngs around the Grove she regretted again the seating arrangement that had separated her from Ernest. If only she had been beside him, she thought. If she had just been able to get one glimpse of him before the fire struck. Now she could not even remember precisely when it was she had last looked closely at him, or what he had been doing. She continued searching through the crowd.

Suddenly she saw a member of her party, Helen Devine, who lived near her in Quincy. Helen's dress was torn, her feet were bare, and she had a gash on her forehead. Marion put an arm around Helen's shoulder and started again to search through the crowd, hoping to find Ernest and the others. But she realized that Helen couldn't stand much more of what she was seeing.

They found Frank Duggan, another neighbour, who told them he was looking for his wife, Mary. Together they continued their anxious search. They gave their names to some reporters in the hope that the newsmen might have run across some of the others in their party, but they learned nothing. When they were asked what had happened to them, they simply could not piece the story together.

At last the sad trio decided that the only wise thing to do was to go home and wait for word of their loved ones there. Not until next day did Marion learn that her husband was dead.

Such was the mood of the people from whom reporters tried to get their stories. They revealed despair, confusion, and anxiety, but few facts. Even the officials had very little accurate information. The fire chiefs, who were friendly with most of the reporters, simply could not take time to talk to them. The politicians, ordinarily anxious to be quoted on anything, were too shocked to compose comments. Mayor Tobin estimated that there might be as many as two hundred dead, but it was clear that this was only conjecture, and that he was emotionally overwhelmed by the disaster.

The reporters telephoned their scraps of information, true and false, to the city desks, which became centres of confusion. Telephones rang constantly, if not with calls from reporters, with queries from anxious citizens. The city editors brushed off the calls from people who were merely curious, but they could not be rude to those who worried about loved ones, even though there was very little hopeful information to give.

Many of the calls came from college officials. Boston is a college city; Harvard, M.I.T., Boston University, Boston College, Wellesley, Northeastern, Simmons, and at least a dozen other colleges had students who might have gone to the Cocoanut Grove that night.

What happened at Wellesley College was typical. Anxious parents telephoned the college from all over the nation. They had heard about the fire over the radio. Where was their daughter?

In most cases, Wellesley officials had no idea. The girls were required to indicate their destinations when they signed out, but these were seldom accurate. How could a girl be sure where her date would take her in the course of an evening? The officials gave the best reassurances they could, then they too asked the newspapers.

But those in the city rooms knew only that there was an

evacuation crisis at the Grove. Even with fifth alarm crews at the scene, and swelling gangs of servicemen volunteers, there was time for very little else but carrying out victims. Any slowdown to answer reporters' queries might cause the death of those unconscious inside the club who might have a chance if they could be brought out in time.

Ambulance routes were now well established, and incoming traffic was barred from all roads leading downtown. Only persons who could prove they were needed at the scene or at a hospital were allowed to pass. Even relatives of possible victims were turned back. A Medford reporter, even though well known to police, had to abandon his car in Charlestown and ride to his office by streetcar.

Police Superintendent Fallon had called in all off-duty men. They were stationed by the hundreds along the roads leading from the Grove to the various hospitals. These routes were kept entirely free of extraneous traffic so that rescue vehicles could travel at top speed.

The firemen began using the four tall windows on Piedmont Street as exits for the litters. The sills of these windows were elevated nearly six feet above the sidewalk, so that every stretcher that was passed through could be clearly seen by the crowd. The gruesome sights did as much to disperse the curiosity seekers as police had been able to do.

At the peak of the evacuation there were close to two hundred men carrying stretchers. The firemen worked inside, separating and extricating victims and passing them through windows and doorways to servicemen and volunteers, who would place the stretchers in ambulances or trucks.

It became apparent that the statistics of typical disasters were to be grimly reversed. In most fires, floods or explosions, the largest figure in the statistics is the number of those who escaped without injury. Next comes the total of those hurt, and last, the tally of dead.

But in the Cocoanut Grove fire, even a rough calculation indicated that there were more dead than injured or unhurt.

Standing in the parking lot, like so many well-trained dogs awaiting their masters, were fifty-three automobiles, most of whose owners would never come out to reclaim them.

A motley jumble of debris had accumulated along Piedmont and Shawmut Streets and on Broadway. There were chairs, stools, settees, handbags, blankets, coats, broken glassware, doors, and overturned tables. Police patrolled the litter to prevent anyone from picking up so much as a charred board as a souvenir of the terrible night.

The stuccoed walls of the Cocoanut Grove were blackened by smoke, stained by dirty water, and spiderwebbed by heat cracks. The roof was full of holes. Every window was broken, and every door either dangled on wrenched hinges or lay flat under the debris. The spectacular façade on Broadway was now a jagged display of broken glass bricks. Every view into the club revealed only blackened chaos.

It seemed unbelievable that this gutted shell could ever have been a swank and sophisticated night club.

But the disorder provided the information and detail to be telephoned in by reporters. Some had a few survivors' names and eyewitness stories, but in general their reports were no more than elaborations on the theme of the brief, shocked calls which the first four reporters had made after one glimpse at the fire.

The first editions to carry news of the fire contained very little more detail in their stories than in their headlines. The *Globe*'s headline read: "Scores Dead in Nightclub Fire. Blaze Levels Cocoanut Grove; 600 Injured Rushed

BY TRUCK, PRIVATE CARS, TO MANY HOSPITALS." The page carried a single fire picture, showing a priest giving the last rites to a victim while an anxious spectator bent over to peer at the face.

By 11.30 the newspapers had their men well organized and were gathering volumes of detail. Denvir, at the *Globe*, had assigned a man to do nothing but listen to the police radio, and to report the destination of every vehicle dispatched by the Police Department.

The dispatcher that night was Mike Powers, a bull-throated Irishman who knew Boston's complex street layout as intimately as a housewife knows her kitchen. Mike's booming voice was heard almost constantly as he devised short cuts for police cars, relayed orders to the men controlling traffic, and plotted the distribution of injured among the hospitals.

Each time Powers sent vehicles to a hospital that had not been used before in the disaster, Denvir sent a reporter to keep a running count of the dead and injured who arrived there. As members of the *Globe*'s day staff arrived, Denvir assigned them to jobs in a clearing-house operation he had improvised. His men made a list of identified dead, a count of corpses known and unknown, a list of injured, a list of missing, and a list of persons thought to have been in the Grove.

At the Grove, Safety Director John Walsh tried to make similar compilations, but most of his people were far too busy to take time for statistics. Finally, Walsh worked out an arrangement with Plakias, the *Globe* reporter, to receive duplicates of the lists which the *Globe* was preparing in the office. In return, he funnelled any new information to Plakias, who phoned it back to Denvir.

The other newspapers worked just as feverishly to cover the story. But the objective of all was something more important than merely beating the opposition papers. It was obvious to everyone that a tragedy of awful proportions demanded the most accurate and thorough report possible.

For Denvir and for the other city editors there was little of the elation that usually accompanied the appearance of a big story in print. The account of the Cocoanut Grove fire was grossly tragic; it gripped even the men for whom tragedy was a familiar routine.

11

AT 11.30 P.M. a harried, disconsolate physician rushed to a telephone at Boston City Hospital and called the police dispatcher, Mike Powers.

"This is Dr. James Manary at City Hospital," he said. "For God's sake, get word over there that they've got to stop bringing us the dead! Aren't any other hospitals taking victims?"

Powers told him that casualties were now being distributed among five hospitals, though at first all had been sent to City.

"I'll send a doctor to the Grove," Manary said. "I want every victim examined for life before he is sent to this hospital!"

City Hospital was now woefully overloaded with dead, dying, and critically injured victims. But fifty-five minutes earlier Dr. Manary had believed he had an enormous advantage in preparedness. His confidence had stemmed from several factors—factors which actually resulted in the saving of many who might otherwise have died.

First, the administrator, Dr. Manary, happened to be present at 10.30 when the first casualties arrived. He had come to the hospital to attend a party in Vose House, the nurses' residence. The party was attended by a large number of off-duty nurses, doctors, and interns. Thus, a large emergency staff was immediately available to handle the crisis.

A sequence of other fortuitous events had brought the hospital itself to a state of unusual readiness. At about 10.10 an elderly man had been brought in, severely burned. He apparently had fallen asleep while smoking in bed. Because of the extent of the man's burns, Dr. C. Winthrop O'Connell, the night executive, sent for Charles C. Lund, a staff surgeon and highly regarded researcher. Circumstance could have brought no person to City Hospital better equipped to cope with the Cocoanut Grove disaster than Dr. Lund.

Several weeks earlier, Lund had been assigned to undertake studies toward the improvement of the treatment of burns. Massachusetts General Hospital had been conducting such a study since the beginning of the year, and Lund had followed its progress closely. His own assignment to pursue a similar project at City came from the National Research Council, which anticipated that burns would be among the most common wounds of war. There was an urgent need for a more effective medical approach to burns. The old method of applying tannic acid had been completely discredited, and the newer method, spraying the burns with antiseptic dyes, left much to be desired.

Because of his research, Lund had left word with the night executives that he wished to be notified of any serious burn cases that came to the hospital. Dr. O'Connell thus called Lund to tell him of the burn victim at about the time the fire flared up in the Melody Lounge palm tree.

Dr. Manary, meanwhile, had left Vose House before the party ended. Instead of going directly home, he dropped in at the accident floor to see if there were any problems. Saturday night was always hectic there, with drunks, car crash victims, and other injured usually arriving at a rapid rate.

Manary and O'Connell examined the burned man, then toured the other examining rooms. They were just about finished when the first victims of the Cocoanut Grove fire arrived. Several of them came in under their own power, and were not badly hurt. Their stories however, gave an inkling of what was to come. Then at 10.31, an ambulance brought in a woman, burned from head to foot, and dead on arrival. From the ambulance driver Manary and O'Connell learned that casualties were being laid out on the sidewalks at the Grove, and they predicted that their hospital would soon receive as many as twenty patients, perhaps more.

Just then Dr. Lund arrived, followed moments later by the doctors and nurses from the party. Although Manary could hear the wail of approaching sirens, he was confident that he and his staff were ready for the emergency.

He knew that the hospital itself was in excellent shape. As part of the preparation for a war disaster, two wards had been set aside for emergency use. They were kept entirely free of patients, and were supplied with everything necessary for handling victims of a catastrophe. On the regular wards, a number of beds had also been kept in reserve.

The first ambulance from the Grove was followed by two taxis, a police wagon, and a deputy fire chief's car. Each carried one or more victims. The living were admitted and sent to Surgery.

But during the brief interval required to examine these patients, the hospital yard filled with trucks, cars, taxis, and ambulances which formed a line that extended on to Albany Street and continued to lengthen.

Manary and O'Connell began examining patients in the corridor on the accident floor, instead of waiting until the victims were brought into examining rooms. As the arrival rate increased, the corridor became so crowded that stretchers could not be brought in. The two physicians worked their way toward the doors, hoping to get the patients moving faster and thus unblock the corridor. Finally they found themselves in the yard, examining only to determine if victims were alive or dead. The dead were sent across the street to the Southern Mortuary, and the living given first aid on the accident floor.

The number of fatalities was fantastic; of the first two hundred Manary and O'Connell examined, life was found in only about fifty. Many of these died on their way to the examining rooms.

It was then that Dr. Manary, his hospital hopelessly swamped, called the dispatcher to order that no more dead be sent.

Still the dead continued to arrive, for they were dying on the way. Both sides of the corridor were lined with litters, some with charred, inert bodies, some covered with sheets, some bearing victims who writhed in pain. Nurses and doctors squeezed past one another in an attempt to tend to the living or to cover the newly dead.

Somewhere among the survivors was Clifford Johnson, not yet identified. He was barely alive. No doctor could have given Johnson more than an hour or so to live. But hopeless as his chances seemed, Clifford was given a blood transfusion and put to bed. Somehow, through all of the rush and desperation, he continued to stay alive.

Up in Surgery, Dr. Lund stopped for a moment to check the status of medical supplies. Manary had designated him medical commander for the emergency, and Lund had given orders that incorporated the basic principles of the new burn therapy, prevention of shock by morphine and intravenous fluids, and sealing off burned areas as quickly as possible.

Supplies had dwindled swiftly. Morphine, whole blood, plasma, saline and glucose solutions, sterile gauze, petrolatum ointment, syringes, needles, oxygen equipment, and bedding had been used up at an incredible rate during the fifty-five minutes which had elapsed since the crisis began.

Ideally, every burned victim would have been treated according to the method recommended by Massachusetts General doctors: cover the burns with an ointment comprised of boric acid in petrolatum jelly, then bandage with fluff dressing and sterile gauze. But patients had arrived at too swift a rate to permit taking the time the new method required. Dr. Lund was forced to revert to the quicker method of spraying the burned areas with triple dye, a fast-drying substance which killed germs and sealed off the burns on contact.

One of Lund's orders was inflexible, however, despite the time required to carry it out. He directed that all burn patients receive intravenous fluids of some kind, preferably blood or plasma. Formerly, burns had been treated as localized injuries. Dr. Lund's order took account of the damage done to the entire body by the burn: shock and blood chemistry change, best combated by early infusion.

Because every operating room in City Hospital was in use, with patients waiting on stretchers outside, Dr. Manary was now sending all incoming patients directly to the wards. The only examination they received on the accident floor was to determine if they were alive. If they were, they were given an injection of morphine and a large "M" was written on their foreheads or chests in lipstick to indicate the narcotic had been administered. Then a needle was inserted into an arm vein and an infusion begun.

The work load was staggering; even the hospital guards were pressed into semi-medical service, helping to lift patients, bringing supplies from remote corners of the hospital, and wheeling the dead to the mortuary across the street. Clerical employees telephoned every absent staff doctor, off-duty nurse, orderly, and intern on file. Private physicians and nurses were also contacted and asked to come in.

Mobile equipment was carried through the long underground corridors to the Dowling Building which housed the accident floor. Against this flow of traffic moved patients on their way to wards in other buildings. Orderlies walked beside the wheeled stretchers holding aloft bottles of blood or plasma that were being fed into the patients' veins. Everyone hurried.

Soon those working on the accident floor took to spraying burns routinely with the garish purple dye, instead of waiting until victims reached the bed wards. The violet stains could be seen everywhere, on bedding, uniforms, and stretchers. But there was no time to consider neatness; doctors were combating one of the most dangerous hazards in medicine: shock.

The body responds to any severe injury, and especially to a burn, by saturating the tissues with protein-rich fluid, much of which it takes from the bloodstream. This thickens the circulating blood and slows its flow, resulting in shock. Unless something is done to dilute the blood and get it moving again, shock becomes irreversible and the victim dies.

Dr. Stephen Maddock, director of City Hospital laboratories, had an excellent weapon on hand to combat this kind of shock—five hundred units of frozen blood plasma, stored for just such an emergency. He and his staff processed this plasma fast enough for a unit to be given each burn victim as soon as a vein could be found through which to feed it.

Shock was not the only crisis facing the doctors. Very early in the emergency the frightful effects of the gases the victims had inhaled in the Grove began to appear.

Patients who seemed hardly burned at all would begin to cough and gasp. Some of them had to have tubes inserted down their throats to keep them from choking. The lungs of others filled up so fast that even tracheotomy—the opening of the throat surgically—could not save them. The inhaled poisons caused the lungs to fill with fluids—a condition called pulmonary oedema. Just as the burned areas on the outside exuded serum, so did the inner surfaces of the lungs. But outside the body the serum could fall away. In the lungs it accumulated; victims were literally drowning in their own fluids.

When it became apparent that a patient without visible burns could suffer and die from oedema, the hospital began to assume that all of the victims had inhaled dangerous quantities of the poison gases. Even the walking patients were put to bed, and each was told to lie quietly, no matter how well he felt, until it could be determined that he was free of the stealthy oedema.

Oedema, shock, and severe burns continued to take a terrible toll. Throughout City Hospital that night, death was the dominant theme. The hospital admitted 129 living patients. The dead-on-arrival numbered nearly 300. Spaced out over the emergency period, the dead and injured arrived at the rate of one every eleven seconds.

At the opposite end of the city, it was the same story, though on a smaller scale: 114 victims were sped over a sealed-off route to Massachusetts General Hospital, regarded by medical authorities as one of the five best hospitals in the world. Of victims taken there, seventy-five were either dead on arrival or died within a few minutes after entering. They died from uncontrollable anoxia resulting from damage to their lungs, or from shock or burns.

This left thirty-nine survivors who were admitted, a number easily accommodated because of studies Massachusetts General had undertaken.

Early in 1942 two research projects had been initiated by the hospital, under contract to the Office of Scientific Research and Development. One was a search for better treatment of infection in wounds. The other was an effort to develop a standard, superior, and simple method of treating burns.

Throughout the year every patient suffering burns was treated in accordance with these studies. The new plan of therapy—the use of petrolatum ointment containing boric acid—was carefully tested and developed. This was the treatment that City Hospital had adopted when it began its own study of burns a few weeks before the fire.

After Pearl Harbour, Massachusetts General's administrative staff had developed a plan by which the institution's full facilities could respond to a disaster of war. By virtue of the burn research and the mobilization plan, the hospital was now ready for the crisis following the Cocoanut Grove fire.

The first patients had arrived at about 10.35. For every four victims sent to City Hospital, only one went to Massachusetts General. Later, when City became badly overloaded, this ratio shifted so that about half of the victims went to Massachusetts General.

Among the thirty-nine admitted alive were Martin Sheridan, the reporter; Buck Jones, Jake Slate, and a young man named Francis Gatturna. Gatturna did not know it at the time, but his wife, Grace, lay dead in the Southern Mortuary opposite City Hospital at the other end of Boston.

The survivors were suffering the effects of burns, partial asphyxia, cold, exposure, fright, shock, and incipient infection. They were wet from the fire hoses, dirty from the soot and grime, and dishevelled from the necessarily rough handling in getting them out of the Grove. Some stared blankly, in stupor. Others raved, screamed, and flung their arms and legs about so violently that they had to be restrained.

One young naval officer, who insisted that the more seriously burned be treated before him, jumped up and down on the accident floor in a futile effort to fight the terrible pain in his burned hands. He died most unexpectedly some time later, and it was determined that the exertion of jumping had so aggravated his pulmonary oedema that it killed him.

There was no one among the thirty-nine who showed evidence of drunkenness. More surprising, in spite of the wild panic that had ensued, no one had suffered a broken bone, and only a few had been bruised.

The night executive had ordered the accident floor cleared of all non-Grove patients. As victims continued to pour in, it became clear that even this would not provide sufficient space. So patients on the sixth floor in the White Building were rolled, in their beds, to other wards. The entire floor was quickly converted into a Cocoanut Grove ward.

Meanwhile, those on the Massachusetts General staff who could not immediately be assigned to medical work were asked to telephone doctors and nurses associated with the hospital.

112

Fire fighters and servicemen join forces to pass a body through one of the high windows on Piedmont Street. (*Photo by courtesy of the Boston Globe*)

Bandleader Mickey Alpert and his singer, Billy Paine, were photographed a few seconds after they escaped from the basement of the Grove. Both had tried to organize the crowd but were overwhelmed in the panic. (*Photo by William Ennis*)

(*Below*) Firemen investigate the remains of the New Lounge on Broadway. (*Wide World photo*)

Dr. Oliver Cope, the endocrinologist who headed the burn project, arrived in a dinner jacket. He was followed by Dr. Nathaniel Faxon, the administrator, who immediately ordered the full use of all phases of the war disaster plan. Faxon's order led to activity in every wing of the sprawling hospital. Emergency equipment and extra supplies were assembled and rushed to the Cocoanut Grove ward.

It is unlikely that a certain patient in a private room in Phillips House, one of the hospital's major buildings, could have remained oblivious to the scurrying of nurses and orderlies on his ward. This patient was ambulatory and convalescent, due for discharge in several days. He had a radio in his room and he was long accustomed to keeping late hours. If he received word of the Cocoanut Grove fire and was able to connect it with the quiet bustle then going on in the hospital, then he—more than anyone else in the building—must have feared the true scope of the disaster.

For he was Barnet Welansky, owner of the Cocoanut Grove. He knew precisely how many extra tables could be squeezed into the Grove's Main Dining Room by headwaiter Balzerini. He knew how many patrons could be herded into his New Cocoanut Grove Lounge. Barney also knew the true capacity of his night club when it was filled, a figure far beyond the capacity stated on his licence application.

The Grove was authorized to accommodate no more than 460 patrons. But Barney knew that he could seat six to seven hundred in the Main Dining Room alone. Two hundred or more could be served in the New Lounge. And down in the Melody Lounge, he could accommodate between one and two hundred. The total was close to a thousand.

Barney knew of the sealed emergency door on Piedmont Street, the locked exit on Shawmut, the inward-opening exit on Broadway, the slow-moving revolving door at the main entrance. Whether or not he thought of them that night in his room is impossible to know, but he suffered a serious reverse in his recovery.

It is probable that some effort was made to withhold from him the full details of the tragedy, since he was a heart patient. It is hard to imagine how he could have avoided a fatal seizure had he learned what actually occurred.

12

IT was nearly midnight. Four young men wearing white hospital uniforms hurried out on to Charles Street, a broad avenue in front of Massachusetts General that was always heavily travelled. The four men, conscientious objectors exempted from military service to work in hospitals, watched the steady flow of cars coming by. They had a strange assignment, and they needed a few moments to determine the best means of carrying it out.

At last there was a space in the line of traffic. The white-clad figures stepped on to the roadway and formed a barrier across the driving lanes. They held up their hands in a signal for oncoming cars to stop.

When the first car halted, the nearest orderly ran to the driver's window. The operator rolled the window down, and the young man spoke. "I'm from the hospital. Will you please help us? We've got to have blood for transfusions." He went on to explain that many Grove victims were in danger of death because there was not enough whole blood to help retrieve them from shock.

The other three orderlies, meanwhile, had stopped other cars and were making the same urgent request. Some of the cars pulled over, and their occupants were taken to a room where an emergency donor station had been set up. Their blood was rushed to the White Building the moment the donation was completed.

On the accident floor, doctors and nurses had formed into teams. Each member had a specific role to perform on the arrival of victims. No patient could be sent to the ward in the White Building until each of these assignments had been checked off.

The purpose of the procedure was to prevent a recurrence of what had happened shortly after the Cocoanut Grove ward was opened. It was discovered that, in the rush and confusion, several dead bodies had been put to bed as patients. The same ghastly mistake had been made in several cases at City.

When it was determined that a victim was alive, his burns were covered with sterile towels and he was given a morphine injection. Clothing was then cut away, and the patient wrapped in blankets. A second check of his heartbeat was made before he was sent to the ward.

Thirty of Massachusetts General's thirty-nine patients had suffered burns. No attempt was made to clean the wounds or to free them of dead tissue, for the burn study had indicated that scrubbing did more harm than good. The burned surfaces were swathed in gauze impregnated with boric petrolatum. Yards of sterile dressings were then loosely wound around the affected areas and fastened with elastic bandages. If limbs had to be immobilized, rolled-up newspapers were used as splints.

The severe damage to respiratory tracts required constant alertness and split-second response by doctors and nurses. A patient might seem to be breathing without effort one minute, and fighting for his life the next. One victim

116

required constant artificial respiration for six hours before he could resume breathing on his own. Five had such badly seared throats that tracheotomy was required.

Every patient on the ward had a needle in his vein at some time. Just as at City, Massachusetts General had had a large stock of frozen plasma available. But, in spite of it, the need for infusible fluid became so urgent that the four orderlies had to conduct their unusual recruitment drive on Charles Street. All over the city, similar efforts were being made. At Red Cross headquarters, thirty National Guardsmen who were scheduled to give blood in a public demonstration on Sunday night to spur donations for the war effort, were rounded up and bled without fanfare.

After receiving blood and fluids, patients could be expected to stave off shock for a while. But another serious danger still threatened: something had to be done to fortify them against infection.

Penicillin, in 1942, was new, expensive, and scarce. At Massachusetts General it was given only to those patients whose situation seemed desperate. Much later, when more was learned about the antibiotic, it was found that the penicillin injections had been far too small to have helped significantly.

For the most part, doctors used an advanced form of sulphanilamide therapy. The disadvantage of the sulpha drugs up until that time had been their tendency to accumulate as crystals in the kidneys. In doses large enough to combat widespread infection there was danger that the crystal formation would stop the functioning of the kidneys, fatally poisoning the patient.

But an infusible solution had been developed that tended to reduce this danger temporarily, and hence make large dosages of sulpha tolerable. Twenty-six Grove patients were given maximum sulpha injections, followed by the special solution. Both dosages were maintained for several days, then stopped.

A burn is considered to be germ free for about two hours after it occurs, because fire hot enough to destroy the skin also kills whatever bacteria are on it, and body fluids can maintain sterility for a time after the skin is gone. To make the most of this sterility, however, great care must be taken that new germs do not find their way to the area after the burn is sustained.

It was impossible to maintain sterile techniques on the accident floors of the hospitals. Patients were being assisted by cab drivers, police, servicemen, and volunteers, all of whom unavoidably brought germs near the open wounds of the victims. Sterilized equipment was quickly contaminated in the process of putting it to use. But germ-spreading or not, the first aid given en route and on arrival was aimed at keeping the patients alive. There was no merit in a sterile wound if the victim died of shock.

Doctors at Massachusetts General had to rely almost entirely on the sulpha drugs to knock out initial infection. Since they could not keep patients on sulpha indefinitely, however, steps had to be taken to eliminate any possibility of reinfecting the burns after the patients reached the ward.

The forty-bed ward in the White Building therefore had to meet the cleanliness requirements of an operating room. Medical equipment was wrapped and sterilized before it was taken in. Nurses and doctors wore surgical gowns, caps, and masks.

At City Hospital, Dr. Lund waged a similar battle against infection, but without the sulpha weapons, which were ruled out because of their toxicity. He relied, instead, upon the antiseptic action of the triple dye, which had been sprayed on most of the patients. He also enforced cleanliness rules for the wards where patients were to be treated.

Nobody was allowed to enter the Grove wards at City unless he had important business. The only exception to this rule was made on behalf of victims about to die. Their relatives, first dressed in surgical gowns, were allowed to make short visits.

Such precautions were vital. Of all the wounds that a body can suffer, a burn is regarded as the worst. Because burns cover large areas, more nerves are involved, causing the broad, violent pain which has no equal.

Surface skin is composed of dead cells, which are tough and dry; tender, maturing cells lie beneath, and under them are cell buds. This triple layer protects the body against infection. But preventing germ invasion from without is only part of the skin's function; it must also prevent loss of fluids from within.

The human body consists mostly of fluids that are constantly shifting in ratio to one another, changing their chemistries to meet the demands of nutrition, respiration, repair of damage, and reaction to disease. Fifty-five per cent of these fluids reside, not in the blood stream, but in the tissues. The retaining wall for these fluids is the skin; when it is destroyed, the fluids will leak out of the body just as water leaks out of a saturated sponge.

Until shortly before the Cocoanut Grove fire, these facts were not generally taken into account in the treatment of burns. Fire and acid wounds were regarded as local injuries involving only those parts of the body visibly affected. Burns were scrubbed with stiff brushes and soapy water to rid them of germs and debris. Tannic acid was applied to create an artificial seal where there was no skin. When the burn was small, these methods proved effective. But if more than fifteen per cent of the skin area was involved, the patient nearly always died. The effects of such treatment upon the entire system were seldom considered.

The pattern of deaths which could occur following burns had been understood only a short time in 1942. A man who did much to analyze them was a staff doctor and researcher at City Hospital—Dr. Robert H. Aldrich.

According to a comprehensive analysis of burns which Aldrich had published in 1938, the immediate threat to a burn victim was death from initial shock. Shortly after the burn, the blood pressure and body temperature fall, the pulse speeds up and respiration weakens. The patient's skin becomes damp and grey. Unless he is given blood or plasma immediately, he will die. The large supplies of frozen plasma and whole blood that Massachusetts General and City had on hand saved many patients from death by initial shock.

In patients who showed no symptoms of initial shock when admitted, Aldrich's analysis indicated that the Sunday punch was coming—delayed shock. This could be anticipated in any patients with severe third-degree burns. They often did not complain of pain, but doctors knew this was only because their burns were so deep that the nerve ends had been destroyed. Such patients, Aldrich said, could appear to be in extremely good condition. But they might be overtaken by extreme shock after six or seven hours, and die before anything could be done. To prevent such delayed shock, doctors not only treated the burns but fortified the patients with several intravenous infusions of plasma and whole blood.

A third threat of death, Aldrich's study warned, was secondary shock, which could be expected in patients who seemed to have recovered from initial shock. After being treated with heat and fluids these patients would rally quickly and show all the signs of recovery. But any time from two to ten hours later they could be disastrously overtaken by shock again.

Because of the threat of these three forms of shock, Cocoanut Grove patients, regardless of whether they seemed to be in good condition, were quickly and repeatedly fortified with fluids until all possibility of shock had passed.

Another danger that Aldrich's paper outlined was toxaemia, the accumulation of poisons in the burns, and the absorption of these poisons by the body. Opinions differed as to whether these poisons were produced by bacteria in the burns, or were toxic materials resulting from the alteration of body substances by the heat that caused the burn. But doctors agreed that, when toxaemia struck, very little could be done.

Finally, there was the danger of infection, to which burns are vulnerable from the moment they occur until they either heal themselves or are covered by grafted skin.

These hazards, plus the harrowing respiratory complications suffered by nearly every patient in the Grove wards, compounded the difficulty of caring for survivors. The night was devoted to a war against death, and the battle required meticulous moment-to-moment care for each patient. Despite Boston's reputation as a great medical centre, the bulk of the burden was carried by only one of its excellent hospitals.

The distribution of injured could hardly have been more lopsided. The 129 patients admitted by City Hospital put an enormous strain on its staff. Yet Massachusetts General could easily have accommodated more than twice the thirty-nine it received. About thirty other victims were thinly distributed among ten other civilian hospitals: Peter Bent Brigham, Beth Israel, Cambridge City, Kenmore, Faulkner, St. Elizabeth's, Malden City, Massachusetts Memorial, Carney, and St. Margaret's.

The reason City received more than all others combined was that accident cases were routinely sent to the city-owned hospital. By the time someone at the Grove realized that no institution could handle so many casualties, it was too late to correct the situation. The problem would have been even more acute if it had not been that most servicemen injured in the fire were sent to military hospitals as soon as they were brought out of the Grove.

Ironically, the other hospitals had made preparations to handle many more patients when they heard of the scope of the disaster. The nun in charge at St. Elizabeth's had received two victims at about 10.40. When she was told of the fire's extent, she quickly organized her staff and facilities. While beds, supplies, and operating rooms were being made ready, she called the police to say that St. Elizabeth's could accept an unlimited number of casualties. But only two more patients were sent there.

Sheriff James Mellen, in charge at the Charles Street Jail, had quickly removed all inmate patients from his infirmary and set up a first aid station. He sent word to the Grove that he was equipped to treat all patients with minor injuries, and suggested that this might take the strain off the larger hospitals. But there was no way for rescuers to diagnose a victim's injuries as "minor," so none were sent to the jail infirmary. Slightly burned victims, like those who first walked on to the City Hospital accident floor shortly after the fire, might easily have been treated at the jail.

City was not only overloaded; its patients also included many of the most critically injured. Consequently, the death rate at City that night was frightful. Many died even before they could be admitted. Of those who expired after being put to bed, the first was Charles Sheehan, of Milton, who died of asphyxia. The second was Charles Stern, whose passing brought to a tragic end one of the most pathetic stories of the fire.

Stern had been in a party of sixteen—one of the gayest in the entire club. The women in the group called themselves "The Allston Sewing Circle." For more than a year they had met weekly in the Allston section of Boston, where they lived, and at each gathering had put a quarter apiece into a kitty. In the weeks before the fire, much of their conversation had been devoted to how they would spend the money. As Boston College extended its winning streak, and the women heard their husbands rave about the team, an idea for a Cocoanut Grove victory party after the Holy Cross game materialized.

In spite of the Boston College defeat, the eight couples had enjoyed themselves enormously in the Grove, largely because of the insistence by the women that they pay for everything. Several parties nearby had enjoyed the kidding to which the women subjected the men. The girls lighted their husband's cigarettes, held chairs as the men sat down, and took charge of ordering dinner and drinks.

They were seated together at a long table in the Main Dining Room. Unfamiliar with the club, they had apparently fled in several directions when the flames entered the room. Only four escaped alive, and Stern's death cut this to three.

Stern's death was one of many, that night and in the ensuing days. Some of the victims never regained consciousness. Others seemed to improve, but were suddenly overcome by fatal oedema. A few with massive burns died in agony.

But for the many who died, there were more who continued to linger, even though everything seemed to be against them. In each hospital, the devotion and intelligence of the staff—and the unbreakable spirit of the afflicted—produced miracles of survival.

But for all of its awful toll in human life, the fire produced a situation destined to teach medical men a lesson of enormous value. The men and women who lost their lives—and those who suffered pain and misery in the hospitals—were to make available, through their sacrifice, knowledge that was to save thousands of future victims of fire.

13

A T 3.42 A.M. on Sunday, November 29, Fire Chief Samuel Pope decided he could no longer keep so many companies away from their stations. The fire was out. The evacuation was nearly complete. So he sounded the "all out"—the order for all fire companies except those housed in the Grove area to return to their quarters.

It had been a colossal mobilization. During the two hours following the alarm the whole city and much of the state had been alerted to the disaster. Every State Guard unit within a thirty-mile area had sent men, vehicles, and emergency equipment into Boston. The Mutual Aid System, by which fire departments in adjacent cities and towns filled in for Boston companies called to the fire, had distributed protective manpower evenly throughout all of the districts.

The Coast Guard, the Navy, the Army, the Air Corps, and the Marines had established individual headquarters in buildings along Piedmont Street. Their senior officers handled the disaster as though it were a battle, deploying men they had commandeered from the area as the situation required.

The management of the nearby Statler Hotel had ordered

its staff to open storage rooms on every floor to provide blankets and sheets for victims. Anyone who had been hurt in the fire, or badly frightened, or who did not want to leave until hearing word of a lost one, was offered a free hotel bed for the night.

The fire departments and military establishments sent in every lighting device that could be spared. When even these were not enough, emergency flares were lighted and set up around the Grove.

About 175 men worked in the evacuation gang, but, even so, it took five hours to remove all victims from the building. Then the blackened rooms were searched again to make sure no one was left.

The stench of burned flesh hung in the air around the Grove most of the night. It became the outstanding impression of those who worked at the scene. It was carried to the hospitals by victims, and back into homes by rescuers who had entered the Grove, and to the newspaper offices by reporters and cameramen who covered the fire.

To newsmen, the fire was the most difficult and fast-moving story they had ever covered. It was especially frustrating for photographers, for few of the pictures they might take were tolerable on the printed page, and the urgency of the situation prevented the posing or selecting of shots. Moreover, they encountered bitter resentment when they tried to take pictures, for the emotions of nearly everyone present were drawn taut; it seemed sacrilege to record such events for publication.

One reporter-photographer team from the Boston *Post*, working in the ambulance yard at City Hospital, was summarily ordered by a guard to stop its work and help carry stretchers on to the accident floor. At Massachusetts General, another news team found its access blocked by a steel fence that the Coast Guard had thrown up to keep out newsmen and spectators.

But such resistance was not wholly justified. The idea of beating the competition and boosting circulation had become secondary to a public service the five papers knew they had to perform—the amassing of specific information for the benefit of anxious relatives and friends of victims.

Most of the newsmen concentrated on finding out names and conditions of victims. The usual feature stories, side-lights, and descriptions were postponed or written briefly, so that major space could be devoted to the casualty reports.

Newsmen were stationed at each of the eleven hospitals and two morgues. Also covered were Waterman's Funeral Home, which began accepting the dead when the municipal morgues became overcrowded; Fort Banks, where military dead were taken; Police Headquarters, where survivors reported those missing; and of course the Grove itself.

As Boston's papers prepared for their final deadlines, the most difficult problem was to estimate the number of dead. Only in a few places were reporters able to count the bodies themselves. Most had to rely on harried officials, who were primarily concerned with the living.

At the Boston *Globe*, lists of dead, missing and injured continued to lengthen. Because of the completeness of its compilations, the *Globe* was designated as the official clear-ing centre for Grove casualty lists. Denvir hoped to publish the names of all the known dead, as well as the correct total of unidentified and missing, in the last "replate" edition.

Word came to the *Globe* of Mayor Tobin's official esti-mate that some two hundred were dead. By then Denvir's running count of bodies, which had been carefully cross–checked by his copy editors, had reached 455. This was the figure Denvir gave to Cutler, his rewrite man, for the first paragraph of the lead story. Denvir intended to add to the figure, if necessary, at the last possible second before the edition went to press.

The night managing editor at the *Globe* was Willard De-Lue, who was apprehensive about Denvir's estimate. The last Boston *Herald* edition he had seen said only sixty were dead, and Boston *Post* headlines made guarded reference to one hundred. DeLue was supremely conscious of the *Globe*'s obligation to report the catastrophe in its true proportions.

"The mayor says two hundred, Phil," DeLue said to Denvir. "I don't think we ought to go above it."

"The mayor!" Denvir bellowed. "What the hell does the mayor know? Listen, I know more about the dead in this fire right now than the mayor, the fire commissioner, and the safety director put together! I've got a count of four hundred and fifty-five bodies! It may go higher before that page goes in!"

The two continued to argue, Denvir defending the figure his men had reported. But DeLue insisted that the *Globe* must avoid exaggerating the facts. In the meantime, *Globe* reporters at each position were adding to the counts they had already given.

The page could no longer be delayed; it had to go to the composing room. Denvir's men had now reported 485 bodies. DeLue reluctantly agreed to an estimate of 450, but refused to go higher. Denvir told his rewrite man to type the larger figure into his story and let DeLue change it on his own responsibility.

DeLue ordered the more conservative figure set in headline type, but did not change Cutler's lead, so the page went in contradicting itself. The 450 appeared in the *Globe*'s largest type. Denvir's 485 was printed in the second line of the lead paragraph under Sam Cutler's by-line. The actual figure probably should have been about 445, for many of the mortally hurt were still hanging on. The error may have resulted from Denvir's insistence on thoroughness—his men were reporting bodies previously tallied elsewhere, moved and counted again.

When the replate editions of the other papers were brought in, Denvir was vindicated. The *Post* and *Herald* had jumped to a figure of four hundred, and a check of names in their lists revealed similarity in sequence and spelling to those the *Globe* already carried.

Two of photographer Bill Ennis' first pictures ran on the front page of the *Globe*'s final edition. One showed a fireman holding a woman's body. The other showed Mickey Alpert, the bandleader, wearing a woman's fur coat, obviously badly shaken by his close encounter with death.

From the moment these final editions reached the street early Sunday morning, November 29, until May 5 the following year, the Cocoanut Grove fire made front-page news. The coverage of the disaster required daily checks with every hospital that had received victims; seldom did one of these calls fail to produce a new story, often another obituary.

More victims died every day. It was December 7—nine days after the fire—before all of the hospitals went a full day without losing a patient.

The Massachusetts dead totalled 410, and the remaining eighty dead brought the tragedy into almost every part of the nation. Twenty-four states and the District of Columbia had somehow sent representatives to Boston, only to be killed in the Cocoanut Grove fire.

By December 8, ninety-one victims remained hospitalized.

One of them was Clifford Johnson, still unconscious but still alive. The newspapers continued to carry occasional obituaries of the others until May, 1943.

On that day, Phyliss Atkins, of Dorchester, gave up her long struggle. She had fought burns of the face, neck, arms, and hands, and suffered from pneumonia, oedema, and anaemia. Every day she had lost more protein through her wounds than she was able to take in. She fought continual pain, fever, and delirium, and died because her attenuated body could tolerate no more. .

She was the last to go.

14

MEDICAL Examiner Timothy Leary wishes to notify the relatives of the victims of the Cocoanut Grove fire that the Southern Mortuary now has six telephone lines open to expedite the identification of victims. The numbers which may now be called are KENmore 6390, 6391, 6392, 6393, 6394 and 6395. He suggests that to spare the relatives any unnecessary unpleasantness it would perhaps be better to give the officials at the mortuary all the details about their relatives which they know. In that way the officials may be able to identify the bodies.

This notice, published in all Boston newspapers, emphasized one of the most appalling aspects of the night-club tragedy: the identification of the dead by their loved ones.

Never before had death accumulated so fast in Boston as it did that Saturday night in November. It would seem that some idea of the staggering total might have been sensed when victims coming out of the Broadway door had begun to fall dead on the sidewalk, or when fire fighters first saw the grim pile of bodies stacked behind the revolving door in the Foyer. But witnesses were consistently shocked and stupefied at the constantly mounting toll,

In the parade of vehicles that left the scene for the hospitals, two had carried the dead and the doomed for every one that bore a survivor. Yet hardly anyone had been aware that the dead were to be numbered in hundreds; each evacuation was made with swift urgency, as though the speed of the vehicle might somehow rekindle lost life.

The makeshift morgues at the scene had been kept active until 1:30 Sunday morning, when the evacuation crews finally caught up with the rapid procession of dead from the burned building. But it was after four in the morning before the last body was taken away.

The custodial responsibility for this ghastly and enormous load of dead fell on two doctors: Timothy Leary, medical examiner for the southern district of Suffolk County, and director of the Southern Mortuary opposite City Hospital; and William J. Brickley, examiner for the county's northern district, whose mortuary stood outside the main entrance to Massachusetts General.

Medical examiners are physicians who seldom escape from their profession. Every doctor expects to be called away from his dinner, his bed, or perhaps even his vacation occasionally. But a medical examiner's career consists of responding to one emergency after another, most of them occurring at night.

Where a general practitioner might tell a patient to take two aspirins and call back in the morning, the medical examiner's patients are always beyond the help of medicine; they must be tended to then and there. If the case involves a felony, as many of them do, a painstaking autopsy must be performed as soon as possible.

With typical dispatch, Dr. Brickley and Dr. Leary had gone to their posts immediately. Leary arrived at Albany Street and Massachusetts Avenue to find that every examining room in Southern Mortuary was crowded with corpses. More were being rolled in through the underground corridor that passed beneath the street from City Hospital. The outer rooms were already crammed with survivors and relatives waiting to be admitted to view the victims.

Leary was shocked to learn that some of the early visitors had been admitted to the horror chambers of the chaotic morgue. His first act was to bring in two of the policemen on duty outside the building. "I want all of these people taken out of here," he ordered. "Nobody is to be admitted to a room containing the dead without written permission from me."

The officers escorted the protesting relatives out of the waiting rooms, then went in to get those who had gone into the examining chambers, but the damage had already been done. Some had fainted, others were hysterical, most were sick. No one had found the person he was looking for.

As more people arrived to search for lost ones, and were barred from the morgue, resentment mounted. Waiting helplessly outside bred anxiety and grief; in their distraught condition, they could not understand the humane motive of Dr. Leary's insistence that no one enter.

Leary was severely criticized for his firmness in keeping everyone outside. One of his critics was Mayor Tobin, with whom he had a public altercation over his handling of survivors and next-of-kin. But Leary stood firm, knowing better than the Mayor the awful effects of exposing laymen to what was inside the morgue.

Probably no morgue in history has ever been so humanely and efficiently organized as the one Dr. Leary set up that night.

After clearing the waiting rooms, he asked the relatives to leave names and descriptions of those they sought. Then he encouraged them all to go home and wait. The morgue already smelled heavily of burned flesh; Leary knew what tragic thoughts the odour would conjure for those who sat waiting in its presence.

Next he buttonholed Eddie Costello, police reporter for the Boston *Globe*. He assigned him to guard the door which led from the main entrance into the morgue chambers. "I can't use a policeman, because the politicians will push him around," he told Costello. "You're the doorman. Don't let anyone in unless he has a card signed by me. I don't care who it is, don't let him in! You do this for me and I'll see that you're first on every identification we make."

The reporter took up his post. Leary headed toward the autopsy rooms, secure in the knowledge that even if Governor Leverett Saltonstall arrived, Eddie would make him get a pass.

Leary then conferred with his assistant, Dr. William Watters. Space was becoming scarce, and everything was in disorder. Both men agreed that a special method would have to be contrived for organizing the morgue. Leary left Dr. Watters temporarily in charge, and went over to City Hospital.

There he talked to Lieutenant May Walker, of Andover, head of the Women's Defence Corps, which was ready to work in any helpful capacity.

"I have the toughest job imaginable for you," Leary told Lieutenant Walker. "I'll understand perfectly if you refuse."

Lieutenant Walker had no illusions; she knew she was talking to the medical examiner, and she knew something of the extent of death in the fire. "I think I know what it is," she said. "We'll take it."

Dr. Leary then explained that the most important job now facing them was to work out a method by which the long sad rows of dead could be identified. "Above all else," he said, "we must be kind. I won't have relatives and sweet-hearts exposed to the shock of passing among corpses. In fact, wherever you can, I want you to eliminate the necessity of survivors looking at any bodies at all."

With this requirement as their starting point, the women went to work. For all of them the assignment was the most singularly repugnant experience of their lives. Some of them had to have temporary relief, but there is no record that any of them quit.

Leary and Watters first arranged for the entire morgue to be partitioned into cubicles made of plywood panels and blankets hung on ropes. Each cubicle was to contain one victim. The only bodies that would be grouped together would be those already identified, and these were to be placed carefully away from any area through which a relative might have to pass.

The women of the Defence Corps conferred with the Red Cross women working in the hospital. They decided to use a filing system by which every clue to identity was put on cards in a triple-reference index.

The hospital had already begun an over-all file for the dead, missing, and injured. The women expanded this by putting the names and locations of all the known dead on pink cards. Green cards indicated those injured and where they were hospitalized. The names of those still missing were listed on white cards.

In addition to this they started another file, using the blue-lined side of the white index cards for descriptions and clues obtained from the unknown bodies in the morgue.

All of the anxious next-of-kin were interviewed by the women in the hospital. At first they asked only obvious ques-tions—name, sex, colour of hair. But as the complaint came back from the morgue that this information was too sketchy, the interviewers made their questions more detailed and specific.

They asked for the shape of the face and the nose; the precise shade and material of a dress. What was the victim's most recent known weight? What was the brand of watch, and what other kind of jewellery was worn?

The hardest to identify, of course, were the women. If they carried any positive identification at all, it was invariably in a purse long since separated from them. Their clothing had exposed more of their bodies to be disfigured by the fire, and their dresses were far more vulnerable to flames than the suits and uniforms of the men.

So the women volunteers, like detectives, cross-examined. What was she wearing to hold up her stockings, a garter belt or a girdle. What was her brassiere size? Make a sketch of her dress, and one of the bracelet and earrings you say she had on. Would she be wearing dress shields? Would she be wearing a half-slip or full length? Where was the placket on her skirt, at the side or in the back? Did she have her toenails painted?

And in the examining rooms in the morgue, Lieutenant Walker and some of the most gallant women ever to volunteer for anything were steeling themselves against nausea and fright to learn such things from the dead themselves.

There were unspeakable things to be done; things May Walker never would have believed she could do without repugnance and terror. But she did them all, and so did the women who worked with her. No one so much as flinched, for they all seemed to know that the slightest personal response to what they were seeing and doing would well up into an uncontrollable outburst.

They learned to lift the eyelids of the dead and to hold them away from the lifeless eyes until someone had a chance to note the colour. They inured themselves to the examination of entire body surfaces, searching for scars, marks, and disfigurements which might help in determining who the victim was.

The professionals working alongside tried mercifully to keep them away from the terribly burned and disfigured. But it became apparent early in the grisly process that these women possessed an invaluable penchant for detail. They would spot such things as dark roots in blond hair, indicating that the woman used a bleach; they would feel under eyebrows for mascara, and determine, if they could, its shade. In some cases they could even identify lipstick hues or the brand of a cologne whose essence still lingered.

Working with them were dentists, doctors, and police. The detectives fingerprinted wherever they could, forwarding the prints to the vast Federal file developed during the period of war mobilization. The doctors looked for surgical scars, medical abnormalities, and features of anatomy that might be known by relatives.

Every scrap of information was listed on the index cards.

The file thickened. Some of the cases became little histories of detail filling three or four closely typed cards.

In the most doubtful cases it was the dentists who were able to identify the lost ones. Tufts Dental School sent over most of its juniors and seniors to take impressions of every mouth. The arrangement of fillings, caps, bridges, and dentures is different in every person; the dentists made charts of everything they found. These were filed with other information from the body, and when a lead to identity was established the practising dentists involved were asked to dig out their records for confirmation

Dr. Albert Murphy, a surgeon, was working with Dr. Watters among bodies so badly burned that no obvious clues to identity remained. He found an abdominal scar on one of them. The suture intervals, the length of the scar, and its placement seemed oddly familiar to him.

He took a scalpel and reopened the incision to study the surgical work and anatomy beneath.

His hunch became a certainty. "I know this boy," he said sadly. "He's Francis Gale, and he lived in Dorchester. I took out his appendix four months ago."

Everybody seemed to understand that, to those who loved him, the finding of one who has died and preparing him for burial is every bit as urgent as giving him treatment when he is hurt. The men and women in the morgue, therefore, worked ceaselessly. To rest was to prolong someone's tortured anxiety; to take food would be out of the question.

Dr. Leary made a public statement very shortly after the gruesome work began. He asked the reporters if they would oblige him to the extent of taking it down verbatim:

"It takes a catastrophe like this one to bring out the fine qualities in people," he said. "I admired these women for their offer, but I seriously doubted that they could face up to what they would have to see and do. Now I know that we could not do this awful job without them."

This was no more than the simple truth. The women continued to note details that would seldom be observed by a man. Where Dr. Leary might describe a dress as "blue," one of the women would add, "turquoise," and discuss the material and style in terms that would be recognizable to another woman. And Leary discovered that they knew a form of anatomy which the medical schools had completely overlooked. They were recording such observations as "recent permanent," "stomach very flat," "wears earrings," and "hips 36, waist 27, bosom 38." Over in the hospital, where next-of-kin were being interviewed, these observations proved to be as germane as the doctors', and sometimes even more so.

There had now accumulated an enormous volume of information to be thoroughly sifted and cross-filed. Leary decided to try, as far as possible, to make identifications through interview rather than by viewing the dead.

The painstaking file bore fruit. The women interviewing were able to narrow down from hundreds of bodies to the one that was sought. In most cases where corpses had to be viewed, the relatives were shown only one—the right one. The women learned to encourage some friend or more distant relative to make the grim visit rather than someone to whom the loss was monumental enough without the added horror of seeing the remains.

The working files became so thorough that a humane rule could be enforced: in no instance was any relative or friend to be required to view more than three bodies. If any of these three involved a badly disfigured victim, Dr. Leary required that the family dentist or doctor make the official identification.

But in those cases where a survivor or loved one had to face the ordeal himself, Leary found again that the volunteers had brought in the wonderful talent of womanliness, which had never graced his institution before.

For they sensed to the fullest the brutal impact of the experience upon those who identified their dead. They knew that, even though there are no degrees in death, the living are apt to impart them in terms of what they see.

So the volunteers sponged away cinders, and invented clever ways to conceal patches where hair was burned or destroyed. They arranged jewellery neatly in place, brushed suits and straightened neckties.

They closed gaping mouths. They tucked clean towels

under heads. With powder and make-up they invented ingenious tricks by which the damage of the fire could be concealed. They fussed knowingly with hair arrangements and mercifully removed the expressions of terror from the features of those to whom it must have been the last emotional response.

In almost every morgue it is the practice to drape the entire body with a sheet that hangs from both sides of a table or slab. The women who worked in Southern Mortuary saw immediately the dreadful connotations of such a sight, and the grim cliché of lifting the sheet back off the face.

So they draped the sheets with their edges resting on the table, bunching the centre so that the stiff outlines of the bodies were softened. They folded the upper edges of the sheets back as they would be folded on a bed.

Because of these thoughtful touches, when a relative approached a victim some of the starkness of death was concealed. The viewer would be aware from the outset that the face was exposed. As he came closer, its detail would gradually become clearer, giving him time to make some adjustment to it.

There was no sudden shock when the sheet was pulled back and the sight of the dead loved one thrust suddenly on his survivor.

Inevitably, with so many dead from so violent a fire, there were bodies which yielded no clue. An ingenious chemist named Frank Stratton, who worked for the city, was called upon to solve such cases. He used certain solutions to refurbish jewellery and military insignia so they would have meaning. With powders and chemicals he was also able to revive colours, identify fabric weaves, and decipher the writing on charred papers.

At the Northern Mortuary, opposite Massachusetts General, Dr. Brickley and similar teams were employing the same kind of detective work. A total of 175 bodies arrived there, seventy of which Brickley had correctly identified by mid-morning on Sunday.

With almost miraculous foresight Brickley had ordered during the week before, one hundred inexpensive coffins to be used in just such a tragedy. After the sad influx began, he contacted the funeral director through whom he had purchased them. The director put four men to work assembling the coffins. Within two hours he sent over enough so that at least all of the women victims could be taken up off the floor before viewers came in.

As the sun rose on the horrified city, hearses began to arrive at the morgues. One of the most shocking photographs of the whole catastrophe was a picture taken outside Southern Mortuary shortly after dawn; it showed fourteen hearses lined up in a black row, the two at the end nearest the building just pulling away.

With daylight came more of the relatives, many of whom had spent the night going futilely from one hospital to another, and had finally resigned themselves to the sad possibility that those they sought were to be found in the grim gathering-places of the dead.

As these relatives made their inquiries, they told sad and ironical stories of how one victim or another happened to be in the Cocoanut Grove the previous night.

Robert S. Murphy, of Cambridge, had been on his way home from work. As he often did, he stopped downtown for a quick drink before tackling the transit system home. But on this night he had apparently stayed for two. His body was identified at the Southern Mortuary.

Lorraine Carlson, eighteen, of Brockton, had gone to the

Grove with seventeen-year-old Robert Noyes, who was among the dead identified early at Waterman's Funeral Home. There was no immediate trace of Lorraine. Her anxious family checked hospitals, morgues, called survivors, appealed to numerous officials. While she was missing, especially as more and more identifications were made, there was still hope that she might be alive.

But she was finally identified, at the place where she had been all the while—Southern Mortuary.

Maxine Coleman, a Grove entertainer who billed herself as "The Best-Dressed Singer in America," was there too, lying dead in only a fragment of the exotic gown she had put on to entertain at the New Lounge.

Robert Widdop, Jr., and his fiancée, Virginia MacCurdy, both of Quincy, were identified in morgues at opposite ends of the city. Dead also were Louise Sullivan and Larry Ford. All four had been together in the Grove to celebrate their respective engagements.

One victim at Southern Mortuary had a man's wrist watch clutched tightly in her right hand. It was identified by Nathan Greer, the Harvard student from whose wrist it had been torn during the frantic escape from the Melody Lounge.

The girl was Kathleen O'Neil, who had made that brief but fatal hesitation at the cloakroom door as the fire raced along the Foyer. She had pulled the watch from Greer's wrist in her last desperate effort to stay with him as he was propelled into the crush toward the revolving door.

On Sunday afternoon, Irving and Betty Soroko went to Southern Mortuary, fearing their suspicions were true. They were looking for Rose Shuman and Albert Rosenfarb, whom they had taken to the Grove the night before. The Sorokos had escaped because of what they now believed to be a miracle, but the other couple was still missing.

The Sorokos' "miracle" was that they had been curious about the New Lounge, which they had never before seen, and had asked a waiter if they could inspect it. They had been shown how to reach the lounge through the service passageway from the Dining Room, where they were seated. Later, when the fire began, it was through this passageway that they fled, with the other couple close behind.

The Sorokos had escaped without injury, but were unable to find any trace of Miss Shuman or Rosenfarb. They were told at Southern Mortuary that both were there, dead of carbon monoxide poisoning.

As the Sorokos turned to leave the morgue they met Barnet Gerson, a friend whom Soroko had not seen since their school days in Chelsea. Gerson told them that his brother, Oscar, whom the Sorokos had chatted with briefly in the Grove that night before, was dead.

"He can't be!" Soroko said. "Betty and I saw him leave—he went out at least half an hour before the fire."

"I know," said Gerson's brother. "But he met some friends at the door and went back in with them. He was found down in the Melody Lounge."

Several days after the fire, an elderly man visited Fire Department Headquarters downtown. He was R. F. Moment, of Newton, and he explained that he had visited or called every known morgue in the city, including the military morgue at Fort Banks and the one at Cambridge City Hospital. Would the firemen please probe the ruins once more? There was still no trace of his daughter, Mrs. Elizabeth Winslow, twenty-six, who had gone to the Grove with her husband, Gilbert. Gilbert had been found at Northern Mortuary.

The firemen obliged. But they found no one in the scorched and gutted Grove.

The distraught father continued his search. Eventually he found his daughter, where she had been all the time—with her husband at Northern Mortuary.

One by one, bodies were claimed and taken away. By the end of the first week, only a few unidentified remained.

In one victim's pocket a letter was found from Private T. H. Murphy of Camp Atterbury, Indiana. The full name of the person to whom it had been sent was hopelessly obscured, but the letter began, "Dear Harry."

Boston police sent a teletype message to State Police in Indiana. Two troopers were sent out to the military camp. Murphy was located and relieved of duty to talk to them. He told them he had written the letter to Harry Hawkins, an assistant steward at the Statler Hotel.

The state troopers sent the information back to Boston. A Statler worker who knew Hawkins went to the morgue and made the identification positive.

By the eighth of December, only one unidentified body remained. So far, the only clue was a door key that had been found in his pocket.

Boston Police checked again the vast file of rumours, reports, requests, and referrals that had accumulated during the long identification process. There was one possibility which seemed worth investigating.

The key from the lone remaining body was turned over to two cruiser officers who drove to 27 Milford Street, in the South End of Boston. They climbed to the second floor, where they tried the key in the lock on Room 23. The lock turned, and the door opened.

It was the final clue they needed.

The last body, which lay in Northern Mortuary, could finally be given a name—Alexander Dashevsky, a part-time waiter at the Grove.

Only the shaft of the revolving door remained after the fire. Beyond is the Foyer, scarred by flames that eventually entered the Dining Room. In the foreground is the stuccoed archway, from which Mrs. George Hayes watched her husband as he struggled to free himself from the jammed revolving door. (*Wide World photo*)

Two members of an emergency evacuation crew search the Shawmut Street side of the Dining Room after the fire. In the foreground are chunks of the false walls, torn out by fire fighters attacking the blaze. (*Wide World photo*)

15

CARING for the 129 patients at City Hospital and the thirty-nine at Massachusetts General was hard physical labour. It involved miles of walking through long corridors, lifting and supporting the weight of patients' bodies, pushing and hauling large pieces of equipment, enduring the constant sounds of agony and the continuing occurrence of death.

There was no end to it.

During that first night at both hospitals, nobody went home. There was no such thing as a meal for members of the staff; even a few gulps of hot coffee seemed almost like plotting against someone's life, for there was always something to be done for the suffering.

But though they worked ceaselessly, the doctors did not fail to record the observations and statistics that were to yield knowledge of what actually had happened to victims in the strange fire.

Doctors at Massachusetts General noted a definite pattern in the distribution of burns among Grove patients. Hands, faces, and the lower halves of the eyes were burned in most cases. Among women, less protected by clothing, there were also burns on the arms, shoulders, back, and legs.

The fact that faces and the backs of hands suffered almost equivalent burns in many cases suggested that these victims, caught in the path of the roaring gas ball, had instinctively raised their hands for protection.

In treating the burns, doctors recorded the precise manner in which they applied the new petrolatum ointment technique. Dressings that were put over burns were left untouched for at least ten days, longer in some cases. Careful records were kept of body temperature and white blood cell count so that, without removing the dressings, it could be determined if burns were infected.

When bandages were eventually taken off, it was found that second-degree burns had healed with virtually no scarring. Third-degree burns had almost no infection and were in excellent condition to receive skin grafts.

Dr. Oliver Cope believed the new technique had vindicated itself completely. It was simple, it involved inexpensive supplies readily available in all hospitals, and it freed the staff to give full attention to the care of shock, anoxia, and the other complications arising from the fire.

The treatment has been standard ever since. Its only refinement has been the addition of antiseptics to the boric petrolatum spread over the burns.

The hospital experiences of Cocoanut Grove victims cannot be understood in summary. Each was different, each excruciating in its own way, and each contributed something to the knowledge of medicine. The Cocoanut Grove fire, in its horrible aggregate of victims, became the most informative single tragedy ever approached by physicians.

The sheer enormity of the work done in the hospitals was reflected by the fact that, during the first two months after the fire, the Red Cross paid for the assignment of 558 special nurses to care for Cocoanut Grove patients. Much of their time was taken up in supervising the many transfusions necessary to keep victims alive.

Some fifteen hundred units of frozen plasma on hand at the time of the fire were used up by the following morning, and a shortage of whole blood began to beleaguer doctors. The Metropolitan Red Cross Chapter appealed to national headquarters for additional blood. A special plane carrying 250 pints was flown in; they were used up before midnight Sunday.

The Red Cross Chapter chairman then called Mayor Tobin and urged him to do anything he could to get more blood. Tobin ordered department heads in the city government to get out and drum up donors among city employees.

At the same time, newspapers and radio stations appealed day and night for blood. Donors responded in droves, but still there was never a time when any hospital had more than twenty pints on hand.

On Monday five hundred donors were processed at the Red Cross blood centre on Boylston Street. Another five hundred gave blood at the hospitals. From chapters and hospitals outside the city came another five hundred. And still the supply stayed only a few pints ahead of the demand. The blood recruiters, who knew there were about two hundred hospitalized victims, simply could not understand where it was all going.

It was going into the veins of victims such as William Shea, who used nine pints the first night. Shea, a huge ex-taxi driver who had become head bartender in the Grove's New Lounge, had been brought out of the fire with burns nearly as grave as those suffered by Johnson. He lay on his stomach in City Hospital, the blankets of his bed stretched over a device called a Bradford frame to keep their weight off his badly burned back. From time to time he would plead to his nurses, "Please, please, get me off my stomach!"

But he could not be moved. From the moment he was admitted, Shea required two nurses attending to his needs day and night. There was seldom a time when he was not receiving something in his arm, through his nose, or in his mouth. His pain was so constant and intense that even large injections of morphine could not assuage it.

The doctors and nurses did their best to keep him alive. Shea himself put up an enormous battle, forcing himself to lie still when every impulse was to thrash out in pain, steeling himself against nausea when the nurses fed him the thick, protein-rich fluids. The excess fat of his 350-pound body did not help much; although he lost more than 100 pounds, the loss consisted of muscle which his body was converting into serum that oozed out through his burns. Shea gave until he had no more to give, and died quietly in his bed.

With Shea, at least death had been anticipated. But one of the young doctors reported the case of a co-operative, cheerful girl who did not seem to be in pain or even in serious discomfort. She was very pretty, and it seemed fortunate that her burns were confined to her hands.

The doctor had encouraged her to call for him or a nurse at the slightest feeling of chest congestion, for by then all of the hospital personnel knew of the drastic oedema crisis that could overtake a victim in a matter of minutes. The girl assured him she needed nothing, and that she expected to be able to go home in a day or two. He could tell she was self-conscious about accepting attention in the presence of patients more seriously hurt than she.

A few hours after her conversation with the doctor, still

without having uttered a single request or complaint, she quietly stopped breathing, a victim of oedema.

But for every loss there was an inspiring win. Al Willette, the saxophone player and boy friend of Pepper Russell, might reasonably have been set aside as a hopeless case so that full attention could be devoted to those who had a better chance.

In fact, when Pepper finally found him at City Hospital, she was sure he had only a few hours to live. Her visit took place between two and four on Sunday morning, when the weight of the tragedy had made any precise notation of time unlikely. In the hospitals, watches were looked at only to count the fleeting pulses; clocks were consulted only to note the hour at which someone died.

Willette's condition was so grave that Pepper was admitted immediately. She was told that he had been given artificial respiration after his arrival, several hours before. He was now breathing on his own, but his chances were very poor.

In addition to the arduous artificial respiration, an intravenous bottle had been attached to his arm, and he had been made as comfortable as possible.

When Pepper looked at him, she saw the bright red lipstick letter that had been put on his forehead to indicate he had received morphine. Pepper, who did not know its meaning, concluded that it marked him among the dying.

She sat beside the bed, sobbing softly, as the nurse told her he had been given the last rites of his church. He was unconscious, and barely breathing. Finally, a nurse suggested that Pepper could contribute nothing by her presence; Willette was so weak that there was no chance of his regaining consciousness. Sadly, Pepper went home.

But Willette continued to survive. Through oxygen

therapy, the repeated pumping out of his throat, the use of humidifiers in the ward, and the unceasing watchfulness of doctors and nurses, he maintained his shallow, almost furtive respiration until his damaged lungs began to clear. Then he started to rally swiftly, and went on to make a startling recovery. He credited his experience in the hospital with enabling him to give up smoking, something he had tried to do for months.

Another patient at City Hospital was in frightful delirium from the time she was admitted. "I'm not dead!" she began to cry out several days later. Then she would lapse into mutterings that sounded like baby talk. Sometimes she would cry out for her mother, "Mother, I'm not dead! I'm not dead!" Then she would become unconscious again.

Although the delirium persisted, the girl's body responded to treatment. She began to sleep, although fitfully, continually plagued by a nightmare in which she uttered the same cries that had characterized her delirium.

When she recovered enough to talk, she told nurses of her terrifying experience at the Grove. "I knew they thought I was dead," she said. "I was squashed into a pile of bodies. I couldn't move or talk. I knew they had forgotten about me. I tried to move, but the only part of my body I could control was one finger. I kept moving it, just a little. I've never done anything that was as hard to do as just moving that one finger."

She had no idea how long she had lain there. She remembered being moved, and that those who moved her had not caught her pathetic signal that she was still alive. For a second time, she felt herself being placed among bodies.

Then she heard someone say, "This one moved—look—she's still moving!"

Desperately she tried to make the tiny motion larger.

Then her eternity of horror was compounded. "They often do that," another voice said. "It's a spasm. She's dead."

But she managed to curl her fluttering finger. Someone lifted her from the pile and determined that she was alive. She was taken from among the dead and sent to City Hospital.

Each patient who survived lived through his own taut drama in a hospital ward during the days, weeks and even months following the fire. Vera Daniels, hat-check girl from the Foyer, underwent repeated surgery by Dr. Charles Lund at City Hospital for the restoration of the skin she had lost. Dorothy Myles, a beautiful radio singer, suffered disfiguring burns which took years to repair.

But there are two accounts of recovery which so uniquely capture the essence of what went on in the hospitals that they deserve to be separated from the tangled chronology of the Cocoanut Grove fire and viewed, from beginning to end, by themselves.

One is the story of Jacob Slate, the Quincy tobacco dealer, who, as he and his wife pressed toward the little door at the left side of the stage, knew that he was falling asleep from the strange, sweet gas he smelled, and was helpless to prevent it.

When Jake woke up in Massachusetts General, he thought his face was covered with caked mud. He also thought he was blind.

Bandages covered his entire head, his neck, his back, and left hand.

Jake was terrified. He cried out and tried to sit up in bed, but when he moved he was stabbed by sudden pain.

"You're all right, Mr. Slate," said a woman's voice. "You're at Massachusetts General Hospital. Try to be quiet."

Jake lay back, still frightened by the unexpected darkness. He heard a hissing sound at the far end of the room; because of the snug bandages, the boric ointment which had been smeared over him, and the excess of humidity in the room, he thought he was in some kind of pressure chamber. Actually the hissing came from steamers which were saturating the air so that patients could breathe more easily.

Jake felt the prick of a needle in his arm. Then he dropped off to sleep.

He awoke violently, feeling that he was choking to death. "I can't breathe!" he cried, but heard his voice muffled in the bandages. "I can't breathe!"

"Take it easy!" said a man near the bed. "I'll get someone."

"Get this off my face!" Jake yelled. "I've got to breathe!"

In the next moment he felt a tube being inserted into his nose. There was a sensation of coolness at one end—it was oxygen, administered by nasal catheter—and he suddenly found he could breathe. He fought back the panic and concentrated on pulling the cool gas into his burned lungs.

The man's voice came back. He said he was a volunteer worker, and he again urged Jake to lie quietly.

After a time the tube was taken out. Jake could breathe now, but his nose and throat felt sore and dry—so dry he didn't think he could endure it.

"Please!" he said frantically to the volunteer. "Will you do something for me? Will you promise?"

"I'll try, Mr. Slate, but you know I can't promise until you tell me what you want."

"I know what I want—I'll die if you don't get it. Please —maybe the doctor will say no. Just get it for me!"

"What is it you want?"

Jake tried to swallow, but the parched tissues would not

move. Again the panic surged up. "Please! A bottle of olive oil. Please!"

He heard the man walk away from the bed. For a long terrible time Jake lay there fighting panic. Then he heard the man's voice. "I have your olive oil, Mr. Slate. The doctor thinks it's a pretty good idea."

Jake groped for the bottle and splashed oil on his forefinger. Then he separated the bandages around his mouth and reached back into his parched throat to paint the sore surfaces. His fingers made him retch, but the cool, thick liquid felt precisely as he had hoped it would. The painful feeling of dryness began to subside. He continued to baste his throat and nose until his pain and panic were gone.

Later, Jake began to think about not being able to see. The thought was so frightening to him that he would not even permit the word "blind" to come into his mind. He knew the doctors would try to break it to him gently; perhaps they might even tell him he would see again. But he couldn't muster the courage to ask if he had lost his sight.

On his fourth day he was told that his wife, Ethel, was dead. So was her sister, and Mr. and Mrs. Caradonna, and Domenic Penardi, all from his party. They were all dead.

And now the doctor would tell him he was blind.

The doctor who had told him about Ethel was still at his bedside. Jake tried to control himself, but he could not. He began to cry as he had not cried since he was a small boy. He sobbed for a long time, then forced himself to say: "I'm sorry, Doctor. I just can't stop."

"Don't you worry about it," the doctor told him. "I want you to cry. Whenever you feel that you must, you go ahead. I don't want you to try to hold it inside."

Jake began to hope that he was burned so badly he would

die. His thoughts kept coming back to Ethel and the others, and to his blindness. As he dwelt on them, the impulse to weep overtook him again. He could not control himself.

He had no interest in the food offered him, nor the medicine his nurses wanted him to take. The only thing he did for himself was to paint his throat with olive oil.

One morning he felt a hand on his shoulder. "Mr. Slate, this is Dr. Kline. I want you to listen to me."

Now it was coming, Jake thought. But he could not just lie there and wait for it.

"I don't want to live!" he cried. "If I can't see, I don't want to live."

He waited for the doctor to say something, but there was silence for what seemed an age. Then he heard Dr. Kline say, "So that's what's been bothering you."

He felt the doctor's hands against his forehead. He heard the crunch of scissors as his bandages were cut away. Dr. Kline said, "Open your eyes, Mr. Slate. Tell me what colour this light is."

A bright, fuzzy light appeared. "Green!" said Jake.

"Now this eye. What colour?"

The new bead of light was smaller, but in sharper focus. "Red!" said Jake.

Jake felt the careful pressure of the doctor's hand on his face, then a large piece of bandage was cut away and Jake heard Dr. Kline say, "Now take a look around, Mr. Slate."

The sunlight was streaming into the ward, and Jake could see it. He looked up; Dr. Kline had a pleasant face, and it was set in an expression he might use on a moderately naughty little boy.

"I thought I was blind!" Jake exclaimed. "I thought I was blind!"

From that moment on his recovery was swift.

In the next few days Jake became a marathon water drinker. He emptied two full pitchers between breakfast and lunch, and another pair in the afternoon. And he ate heartily.

Dr. Kline often made his rounds with a group of medical students. He would say, "I want you to meet Jake Slate. He's the world's champion water drinker." Then he would impress upon the students how important a part of therapy the water drinking had been.

Dr. Kline also praised Jake for the olive oil treatment, although he told the students to use medical oils instead.

When Jake's bandages were finally removed, his burns were almost gone. His face healed without a mark. Jake left the hospital after four weeks.

Another patient admitted to Massachusetts General was thirty-year-old Francis Gatturna, of Roslindale.

Gatturna and his wife, Grace, had been sitting in the Main Dining Room near the stage when the fire struck. The toxic smoke reached them quickly, and Gatturna lost consciousness.

When he came to, he was lying on a blanket on the Shawmut Street sidewalk. Two firemen were giving him artificial respiration. One applied pressure to his back while the other administered oxygen from an inhalator.

Gatturna arrived at Massachusetts General in better condition than most. His face had been slightly singed and he had a second-degree burn on his knee, but less than four per cent of his body was burned. His throat was sore, but he was not in shock.

He was put to bed and given a sedative. During the next ten days he had a fairly uncomfortable time with his congested lungs and sore throat, but his condition was never critical. On the fifth day it was decided that a Red Cross worker should tell him of his wife's death.

Gatturna seemed almost relieved to learn the facts. "I guess I knew it," he said. "If she was all right, you would have told me when I came in."

During the next few days he was quiet and depressed, but seemed to brighten a little as the time came for him to go home. When he left the hospital it was felt that he had made a healthy adjustment to his loss.

Gradually, at home, a pronounced change developed. Gatturna could not sit still for more than a few minutes. He would bolt out of a chair, pace rapidly through the house, then sit down in a different chair. The longer he stayed inside, the more restless he became. Frequently he would put on his coat and walk swiftly but aimlessly around the neighbourhood.

His family suggested he take a trip to visit relatives—just for the sake of the change that seemed so imperative. Francis did not express much enthusiasm for the idea, but he went anyway.

The trip did not help. He returned even more agitated than before. When his family tried to talk to him, he seemed oddly pre-occupied. Sometimes they doubted that he heard what they said. He was obviously frightened of something, and there was no way to make him tell what it was.

By the first of the year his mental state was so alarming that his parents brought him back to the hospital.

Psychiatrists Stanley Cobb and Erich Lindemann talked to him. They found him totally unresponsive.

"Nobody can help me," he would say. "When is it going to happen?"

Enormous patience was required to make him say more. He told the psychiatrists he felt a tension within himself that was at times unbearable. "Sometimes I can't breathe," he said. "I'm doomed, aren't I?"

No matter how much he rested, he complained that he was weak and exhausted. "Something terrible is going to happen to me—I know it," he would say.

Then he was overtaken by a drive to tell, over and over, what had happened in the Cocoanut Grove. "Grace wouldn't come out with me. I started for the door, then I went back to get her. But I fainted. I couldn't get through the crowd. She was burned and I was saved. I should have saved her, or I should have died too!"

Now the doctors knew where they stood; Gatturna was a victim of his own accusations of guilt for his wife's death. His psychosis was similar in pattern to those beginning to appear in servicemen—especially flyers—who had been exposed to violent combat, and who often blamed themselves for the death of a friend.

The doctors tried repeatedly to convince Gatturna that he was not guilty of his wife's death, but he would not listen. He would begin muttering, repeating the story of his escape as though he thought they had not understood it. As he recounted the tale, his body vibrated with fear.

Gatturna was given sedatives at night, but he could not sleep. He spent most of the night muttering and trembling in his bed, shifting from one posture to another.

The doctors gave instructions to everyone on the ward that he was to be closely watched.

More interviews were attempted, but Gatturna's resistance increased to the point of open hostility. Then, abruptly, his mood changed. He became calm. He responded to his doctors. He seemed to feel that at last they were beginning to understand him. He even made an effort to play ping-pong, although he soon lost interest in the game.

A special nurse had been assigned to him after he exhibited extreme depression on the third day. At first she had found him sullen and hostile. But on the fourth and fifth days, when his change in mood was observed, he seemed to make a positive effort to be sociable toward her, as if to atone for his earlier rudeness.

On the afternoon of the sixth day, Francis seemed greatly improved. He initiated a conversation with his nurse—something about how brightly the sun seemed to shine on a very cold day.

He pointed out a large patch of ice drifting down the Charles River and suggested that it had almost the shape of the continent of North America.

The nurse looked down over the Esplanade to study the ice pattern. From that height the patch did seem, vaguely, to have the shape he suggested.

Then there came a sudden rush of footsteps beside her; she saw a swiftly moving figure to her left. It was too late to stop him. There was a crash of glass, a terrible scream, then silence.

Francis Gatturna had paid the debt he believed he owed his wife.

16

AMONG the Cocoanut Grove patients in hospitals, the most critically burned was Clifford Johnson, the twenty-year-old Coast Guardsman. No human being then known to medical history had ever survived such damage.

Johnson was the farm boy from Sumner, Missouri, who got out of the fire unharmed, the first time, but went back inside to save the girl he had dated that evening. He never found the girl, but he did help others to escape.

He went back inside four times. On his last trip out, he was completely wrapped in flames. When he hit the sidewalk his burned flesh was rasped and scraped by its rough surface. The rush of pain was so terrible that he fainted instantly.

When he arrived at the ward the nurses began stripping away the remains of his charred uniform and underclothing. Clifford was so terribly burned that they could not tell where the clothing ended and his flesh began.

The sight of him was gruesome, even to those accustomed to viewing damaged bodies. It was obvious that this boy was mortally burned, and that anything done for him could be no more than an obeisance to chance. Why his heart continued to pound and his blood to flow was a mystery.

But it would not last long, they all agreed. It couldn't. Already they were losing victims injured far less seriously than he. His entire back, buttocks, and legs were charred. The flesh was burned away to the kidney on his right side. The blackened wounds extended around his torso, so deep in one place that the ends of two ribs were exposed. His thighs were roasted, the left one down to the bone above his knee. A burn on his chin exposed the jawbone.

Nobody had ever before survived with more than twenty-five per cent of the skin of his body burned away. Less than half of Clifford's skin remained.

It seemed just a matter of going through the motions until his heart gave out.

He was unconscious and in deep shock. His pulse was rapid and weak, his breathing barely detectable. His burns were so extensive that there was no place on his body where blood pressure could be measured.

The first treatment of his burns was the triple dye, sprayed liberally over the exposed tissues. Then he was put into bed on his back. The nurses managed to find a usable vein in his arm, and began giving him the first of the seventeen pints of plasma he was to receive that day.

Then Clifford got his own private doctor.

Philip S. Butler, a Tufts medical student in his final year, had a clerkship at City Hospital. This was a category between that of the ordinary medical student and the graduate intern. Butler was assigned to stay with Johnson and keep him going—if he could.

Theoretically available to Butler during the next four days was the advice and assistance of the entire medical staff of a great hospital, plus that of a swelling number of

These cars, parked next to the Grove on Sunday morning, belonged to patrons and employees who had died or were injured in the fire. It was the duty of police to trace their owners. (*Below*) Police and fire department officials inspect the Shawmut Street side of the club, where Safety Director John Walsh helped scores to escape. (*Wide World photos*)

Following the fire, a crowd gathered outside Southern Mortuary as relatives waited for word of their kin. Dr. Timothy Leary, medical examiner, was severely criticized for refusing them immediate entry, but his motives were entirely humane; few of the anxious relatives could have endured the grim scene within (*World Wide photo*)

specialists and practitioners who had come in for the emergency. But in practice Butler was almost entirely on his own, for the other doctors all had heavy loads to bear in the crisis. Clifford was conspicuously a hopeless case; they owed their best attention to the others.

Butler's battle to save Clifford was a moment-to-moment affair. In attending his patient he went almost entirely without sleep for the next three days. It was a frightful vigil in which he seldom knew whether Johnson's body responded to or rebelled against what he did for him. He kept the boy alive by ingenuity, devotion, and buckets of intravenous fluids. In addition to the seventeen pints of plasma that Clifford was given during the first twenty-four hours, he received 3,000 cc.'s of saline solution. Before each infusion, Butler had to search over the burned body for a vein which would accept the needle.

Butler resprayed Clifford's burns several times in an effort to build up a crust solid enough to hold back the relentless seeping of fluids from the exposed tissues.

All the while, the signs of life kept weakening. Johnson's temperature dropped to the low nineties. What skin was left became grey and clammy. He could have died any second without surprising anyone.

But he hung on.

This was no display of courage or will to live—not yet. Johnson was just about as deep in the unconscious state as a human can go without slipping into death. What was happening now was that a magnificent body was responding to the terrible disaster which had overtaken it, clinging to life by chemistry, unconscious will, and, as many believed, divine power.

It wasn't until the fourth day that the activity in the hospital slowed down enough to permit any of the staff to take a serious, uninterrupted look at Johnson. By simply staying alive that long in spite of his woeful injuries, Johnson had won himself the right to be the subject of an earnest conference among three of the top doctors.

They were Dr. Lund, who had been directing the medical treatment of Grove victims at Boston City Hospital; Dr. Robert H. Aldrich, who probably knew more about the treatment of burns than anyone in the country at that time; and a general surgeon named Newton C. Browder.

Dr. Browder was an easy-going man who seemed to regard the practice of surgery as a sort of handy-man's trade involving people. But those who had seen him work knew that he was devoted to his job in the same way Brahms was devoted to music. He was what his fellows described as "a damned good surgeon".

Following the fire, Dr. Browder had worked for thirty-six straight hours like everyone else. If he had seen Clifford Johnson at all in that time he didn't remember it, and he certainly didn't associate a name with him. To Browder, Clifford could only have been a boy so badly hurt that he had already lived beyond his time.

But here he was, still alive.

Browder studied Clifford's wounds and read the dismal chart. Everything he saw and read indicated that the boy was dying. It was almost unbelievable that Butler and the nurses had kept him alive so long.

Dr. Aldrich examined Clifford too. But when he was finished, he told Lund and Browder, "We can save this boy. I mean it. If we handle him properly, he can make it."

Browder looked down at Clifford. He pondered whether there was any real hope of making this boy survive. But he knew that Aldrich was not a man to speak without conviction. Aldrich had already been the spark of several stormy controversies, but there was no question in Browder's mind of his authority concerning burns. Browder knew that if Aldrich thought this boy could actually be pulled back, repaired and made sound again, that opinion had solid intelligence at its base. That was enough for Browder.

They had turned Johnson off his back for the examination; now they decided not to turn him again, because of the massive destruction there. Browder estimated that forty-five per cent of Johnson's skin was lost in third-degree burns and fifteen to twenty per cent in second-degree. The one thing in Johnson's favour was that he apparently hadn't breathed much of the noxious gas that characterized the fire, for there was no evidence of the pulmonary oedema that was killing so many other victims.

Dr. Browder's first step was to move Johnson to a four-bed ward in the Dowling Building. He was the only patient in the room. The rest of the space was taken up by the sterile supplies, surgical equipment, and medications he needed.

The Red Cross assigned and paid for six special nurses a day to take care of Johnson. They worked in pairs, for shifts of eight hours. Those were eight hours of hard physical labour. Every minute there was something to do for Johnson —whole blood transfusions, plasma or saline infusions, pulse and respiration checks every quarter hour, food by stomach tube. Clifford's system kept sending serum out through his burns so that his body dripped like a saturated sponge. He required stacks of fresh bedding every day.

Dr. Browder, usually with Dr. Lund or Philip Butler, examined the burns minutely each day. It took the better part of an hour to pore closely over every square inch of burned area. Every pocket of infection had to be found, cleaned, and resprayed with the garish triple dye.

Although by this time the boric ointment treatment was almost universally employed throughout the hospital, Dr. Browder continued to use the triple dye on Clifford in the hope that it would help build up the granulation tissue which he had to have before the doctors could begin grafting. Another reason for the use of the dye was that the boric ointment treatment required dressing, and Clifford was burned too massively to be bandaged.

During the whole month of December the closest Johnson ever came to consciousness was wild delirium. Most of the time he was in a state compounded of sleep, unconsciousness, and shock. If he rose above this state he was brutally sent back by assaults of terrible pain.

Hovering over him for hour on endless hour was Philip Butler, employing all of his freshly learned knowledge of medicine, following the advice of Browder and the other doctors, and improvising whatever else was required.

One of the routine medical chores he had to perform was to give Clifford shots of codeine to cut down the pain. Dr. Browder had taken Johnson off morphine at the beginning. The codeine was milder, but Clifford had to have so much that Browder and Butler knew he would become severely addicted and would demand it even when the pain was gone. But there was no choice. When his suffering became intense, Johnson would soar off into frightful shock, his pulse rate shooting up so high that it couldn't be counted.

Dr. Browder and Butler could not understand how this Missouri farm boy kept going. Nearly every day he would overcome a major crisis of one sort or another. He was losing more protein in his urine alone than they were able to get back into him, to say nothing of the protein which continually wept out of his burns as serum. They couldn't

164

weigh him, but they could see the relentless shrinking of his body as his chemistry converted muscle tissue back into liquid protein for use in basting his burns.

On top of all this, there was infection.

Although almost any kind of germ could be found in Johnson's burns, Dr. Browder felt he could not risk the use of sulpha drugs. Clifford would have had to be put on a daily diet of sulpha to hold down the infection, and his kidneys would most likely have been cut to pieces by sulpha crystals.

So Browder fought the infection by cleanliness, the chief feature of which was the arduous daily session of poring over Johnson's body, searching for pockets of germ colonies in his flesh, patiently cleaning them by hand, then spraying him with the triple dye.

Everyone in the hospital laundry knew Clifford's bedding when they saw it, even from a distance. This was because of the garish purple triple dye, which would never be washed out of fabric it had touched. Rather than continue the permanent staining of more and more hospital sheets, the laundry washed and sterilized the ones already stained and sent them back to Clifford's room.

Nobody was allowed in that room without mask, cap, and gown, or with the slightest symptom of a cold. Dr. Browder and Butler scrubbed up and put on sterile gloves every time they touched their patient.

In addition to the constant threat of death by shock, they had watched for the symptoms of toxaemia, the poisoning which Aldrich believed might result from the absorption of toxins produced by germs in the burns. Toxaemia reaped a terrible harvest among Cocoanut Grove victims, and it had seemed certain that Clifford could not avoid it.

And he did not.

He developed toxaemia in one of its worst forms—haemoglobinuria.

This condition resulted from blood cells which had burst open or shrivelled up when exposed to the heat of the fire. When the accumulation of debris became too great for the system to handle, the haemoglobin would be picked up by the kidneys and appear in the urine.

Fourteen patients at Boston City Hospital had developed haemoglobinuria before it struck Clifford. Every one of them had died.

There was nothing for the doctors to add to the treatment Clifford was already receiving. By now they had developed an attitude half of faith, half of resignation, toward Clifford's ability to stay alive. But this time the statistics were one hundred per cent against him. He simply had to die.

Dr. Browder and Butler stayed very close to him as the condition worsened. Measuring his various ebbs and flows as best they could, they would give him a transfusion of fresh whole blood, or increase the portions of protein he took by stomach tube, or attempt whichever of the other fluid infusions seemed most urgent at the moment.

Clifford had already received a stupendous number of blood transfusions, but they continued to pour more blood into him. Any one of these transfusions could have given him hepatitis or some other undetectable blood infection, but his need outweighed by far any such risks. He had been regarded as dying many times before, but this time it seemed inevitable.

Slowly the foreboding colour began to fade from his urine. The measurement from one analysis to another showed a barely perceptible decrease—so slight as to be hardly significant. But finally it disappeared. Clifford continued as before

—infected, unconscious, losing weight, running a fever, his raw flesh weeping serum.

But he was still alive.

Day after day he continued to hover. Then, just before Christmas, Dr. Browder became aware of another crisis. But this time, at least, it was one not involving Clifford's physiology.

It was the special nurses. Clifford was wearing them out as a racing car wears out tires.

Most of them were young graduates who could be dispassionate only toward moderate suffering. But to work for eight straight hours over this pain-wracked, half-destroyed body was too great an assault on their sensibilities. In his deep delirium Clifford often sobbed like a child, and if he came to partial consciousness it was to moan and cry out against his pain.

None of the nurses quit, but their response and sympathy made them useless. Dr. Browder would come in to find them sobbing, near collapse, still trying to minister to Clifford, but so close to breakdown as to be dangerous to him. Browder had no choice but to relieve them and send for someone else.

On the day before Christmas there was nobody left. The only nurse the Red Cross registrar could think of who could handle Clifford had just finished twenty days with two other badly burned Grove victims. It seemed doubtful that she would be willing to give up her holidays to take on so depressing a case.

But the registrar called anyway. She told the nurse frankly what she would be up against. Further, she told her she was to take the seven-to-three daytime shift, the most active period of work.

The nurse grumbled, but she did not refuse to come in.

She said she'd be there as soon as she could get into a fresh uniform.

Thus did a nurse named Mercy Smith come to work with Clifford.

Mercy was in her middle thirties. She was a graduate of the nursing school at Massachusetts Memorial Hospital which indicated she had received exceptional training. When she worked she was likely to wear an expression that was something between a pout and a scowl; her patients got the impression she was all business, no nonsense, and swallow it down quickly, please. But if she could be provoked into a smile the patient could not fail to notice how naturally it fitted her features, and how completely misleading was her crust of peppery impatience.

And Mercy knew her business. Her career had consisted almost entirely of giving special care to the seriously ill, and it had made her a petite bundle of crisp efficiency. Her heart went out to her pathetic patient the first time she looked at his horribly mutilated back, but instead of reducing her to useless tears, it toughened her to do what had to be done devotedly if he were to live.

Mercy Smith, Newton Browder, and Philip Butler (who presently went back to his classes at Tufts but spent all his spare time with Clifford) toiled over their patient every day, seven days a week. They were by no means alone, for by this time the whole hospital and most of the city were rooting for him. But they were closest to him when he was closest to death. They came to know him and each other as intimately as though they were all of a family. Caring for Clifford became a conspiracy against what looked hopelessly certain every day.

Mathematically, the boy seemed doomed. The simple

measurement of the protein he was losing against the little they were able to replace indicated that he was devouring his own body. Late in February this process reached its inevitable conclusion. He had lost more than sixty pounds. His blood was thin and watery. He ran a fever most of the time.

The Red Cross brought his mother and father on from Sumner to be near him when the time came.

What made it worse was that Clifford was consciously working with the doctors now. He had started showing signs of awareness in the middle of January.

It could not be expected that, when Johnson became aware of what had happened to him, he could entertain any more hope for himself than those who were watching him die. His pain was monumental, his body destroyed. The simplest exercise of intelligence suggested that death might be preferable to the frightful ordeal he faced.

But Philip Butler argued urgently against this attitude. He would sit by the side of Clifford's bed and talk endlessly. These were private conversations in which Clifford made few responses. But he listened. And in the mumbling monotone Butler kept pouring into him all manner of propaganda on the importance of staying alive.

Mercy Smith heard few of the words, but she understood the message. The impact of the intimate communion between these two young men, one trying to be a doctor, the other trying to be no more than a mortal, touched her more poignantly than the knowledge of Clifford's pain.

It was unbearable to watch him die in spite of his colossal effort. In every other crisis there had been something definite to be done—another transfusion, respray him, break up the infections, bring his fever down.

But now these were merely part of the routine—there was nothing new or special they could attempt.

Their helplessness was caused by his intake problem. His main nutrition was Amogen, a protein concentrate which they gave him intravenously, and a milk protein concentrate which he drank. Mercy Smith tried to cook dishes that were tasty to him, but even when he was enthusiastic about their flavour he lacked the strength to eat enough to do him much good. Every measurement they made showed an increasing protein deficit.

They boosted his protein intake to the maximum. But here, too, they were frustrated by the threat that too much would cause a diarrhoea that would cost them more than they gained.

At the beginning of Clifford's twelfth week the protein cycle headed into its logical conclusion. Dr. Browder conferred with Dr. Lund about the worst of all the crises: Clifford was developing oedema.

His tissues were becoming saturated with fluids, because the loss of protein from his blood allowed fluids to seep out of the blood vessels. He was swelling everywhere, even where there were no burns. Dr. Browder had tried to eliminate the monstrous leg swelling by elevation, but with no success. The watery consistency of Clifford's blood had reached a point which the medicine of that day regarded as irreversible. At last he must die.

Dr. Lund recognized the inevitability of Clifford's protein pattern as well as Dr. Browder. But now he learned of one more effort that could be made.

At that time, Dr. Edwin Cohn, a brilliant biochemist at Harvard Medical School, was beginning the development of plasma fractionation, a process by which the various proteins in blood plasma could be separated and used or preserved individually. Cohn had already learned that serum albumin, one of the first proteins to come out in his fractionation process, controlled the viscosity of blood and the ratio of fluids in the body tissues to fluids in circulation.

Cohn was preparing units of serum albumin for the Navy, to be used in cases where deep shock had to be reversed without overloading the system with the other blood elements. In order to make one unit of this serum albumin. Cohn had to have eighteen pints of whole blood.

Dr. Lund wanted to get some serum albumin for Clifford. To do so he had to cleave through complicated resistance in wartime Washington. He emerged from these struggles with nine units, which he gave to Dr. Browder.

Dr. Browder did not know, when he gave Johnson these units, that serum albumin had recently been tried as a desperation measure on two cases who had also suffered the massive oedema that was killing Clifford—and that both these patients had died. Had he known, he would not have administered it to Johnson.

Over the next three days Browder gave Clifford seven of the nine units. After the seventh the ratio of Clifford's albumin to globulin suddenly reversed, suggesting that his body was not tolerating the infusions. This was considered a serious danger signal, and Browder had to stop.

Now there was nothing to do but wait.

Clifford was unconscious again, running a wicked temperature. His pulse fluttered faintly. He could die any second now.

But he did not die.

Instead, the frightful oedema began to subside. Dr. Browder could almost see the tissues shrink back over the next twenty-four hours. The swelling disappeared completely. Tests showed that Clifford was retaining the protein concentrates. For the first time since he entered the hospital he was taking in more than was oozing out.

Dr. Browder said he was convinced that this case was under the personal supervision of "the Man uptairs." No other explanation made sense.

Clifford's comeback from the oedema was breathtaking. The boy who had been so nearly dead was suddenly in such good shape that Dr. Browder began planning to start skin grafts.

Ordinarily Browder liked to begin grafting a week or two after the burn. But this had been impossible because Clifford was in so continuous a state of crisis. Yet now he had developed excellent surfaces to receive transplanted skin.

Often a burn is followed by what surgeons call "exuberant granulation", much of which has to be cut out and allowed to mend before grafting can be expected to take. But nature had distributed blood vessels and fibrous tissues through Clifford's burns so neatly that Browder saw very little that had to be cut away. Within a week Clifford Johnson was ready to receive the tiny spots of skin which, it was hoped, would grow toward each other and cover him again.

For the first surgical session, Dr. Browder and his team scrubbed up and dressed right in Clifford's room. To move him to surgery could have meant irreversible shock, in addition to the probability of riddling the operating room with the virulent organisms that grew and thrived in Clifford's burns.

Dr. Browder was assisted by two of the staff doctors and two nurses. A third nurse scrubbed with him. After soaking Clifford's back with saline-saturated sponges, they draped him, gave him a strong shot of codeine, and administered a local anaesthetic in the arm which was to supply skin for the grafts.

Dr. Browder picked up the grafts himself. Using a curved needle which had three cutting edges, he would take up and cut away about a millimetre of skin from Clifford's arm. The needle would then be passed to his assistant. The assistant would take the needle in a Kelly's forceps and hand it to the third surgeon, who would place the tiny skin patch down on Clifford's back. Each millimetre of skin was given about a centimetre of area to grow in.

There is no more arduous, painstaking form of surgery. The grafts would stick to the needle, or slip out of position after they had been put down. In three to four hours the team planted anywhere from 1,500 to 2,500 of the grafts. Then Clifford's body began to rebel. His pulse shot up again, and they had to stop.

About three hours after the session Dr. Browder took a piece of very fine-mesh gauze—about as tightly woven as shirting material—and cut it to fit the area he had just grafted. He placed it on the burned area with fresh collodion, making it stick down as snugly as he could.

Then he put a fluff dressing on top. Over the bleeding donor site he sprayed a coating of the triple dye.

Dr. Browder had given Clifford a pint of fresh whole blood before the first session in the hope that it would help the grafts to take. But he had resigned himself to the probability that half or more of the precariously located spots of skin would slough off from infection, float off from oedema, or rub off through irritation.

He asked the nurses to keep the fluff dressings soaked down with saline for the first day. The donor site had already hardened over nicely, and Clifford told him it had stopped hurting. Browder decided to stay with the triple dye throughout the grafting sessions.

On the tenth day Dr. Browder went in to see how many of his first grafts had taken. He lifted the fine gauze carefully, almost afraid to look underneath. It was entirely possible that everything he had put down would be stuck to the gauze. If luck had been with him, perhaps as many as thirty per cent of the grafts might have taken.

But the gauze came away neatly. More than ninety per cent of the grafts were seated perfectly and beginning to grow outward toward each other.

The incredible Clifford Johnson had come up with another miracle of healing.

Dr. Browder and his surgical team-mates cheered as though one of them had just won the sweepstakes.

They went ahead enthusiastically with the grafting of Clifford's back, slowed only by the scarcity of sites from which to take the pin-points of skin. As each graft began to grow, Dr. Browder would have the nurses treat it with a seventy-five per cent cod liver oil preparation. He found that this stimulated the growth of the grafts and of the granulation tissue on adjacent ungrafted areas.

Before one of the surgical sessions, Dr. Browder was prevailed upon to omit the transfusion of whole blood. This was the only time the grafts failed to take. From then on he insisted upon whole blood, as fresh as possible, before attempting any grafts.

If Clifford Johnson did indeed have God working for him, He worked through incredibly capable human assistance and devotion. Mercy Smith tended the new grafts with nun-like dedication, changing the fluff dressings and spreading on the cod liver oil preparation with sterile throat sticks, and tirelessly keeping Johnson clean and comfortable. Phil Butler came in every day, strengthening and broadening the bond upon which Clifford now depended. Browder and his surgical team worked with patience and skill at their arduous, seemingly endless chore of grafting.

Everyone in the hospital, it seemed, had some kind of

suggestion for helping Johnson make it. Dr. Browder listened to them all; those that made sense, he tried.

One idea was that ultra-violet light might help the skin grafts to take. Dr. Browder blocked off a test area of newly grafted skin and exposed it to the artificial sunlight for thirty seconds each day. He found that the treatment toughened the grafts and seemed to stimulate their growth. Also, he knew that the ultra-violet was helping to kill off some of the germs that still thrived in Clifford's exposed tissues.

Another suggestion concerned Clifford's bone infections. In addition to the three that were caused by the direct exposure of bones in his deep burns, Clifford developed a fourth as a result of prolonged pressure in bed.

An osteomyelitis, as bone infection is called, is a stubborn colony of germs which finds a vulnerable spot in the thin tissue covering the bone, and stays there—sometimes for years. Once established it's uncertain whether such colonies are ever knocked out completely.

Dr. Browder knew he had to prevent any more from developing, and that bed pressure could cause them. It was suggested that he experiment with a method of improving circulation in bed patients by creating mechanical motion in the bed.

Browder was able to obtain a machine consisting of a complex system of air pumps controlled by an electric timing mechanism. He connected the pumps to a series of inflatable blood-pressure cuffs which were placed across Johnson's bed, parallel to each other, under the sheets. The timer would cause one set of cuffs to inflate for one minute, then deflate. Alternately the other set would inflate. In this way no part of Clifford's body was ever subjected to pressure from his own weight for more than a minute. During that minute his own circulation would tend to prevent the accumulation of germs at any point on his periosteum—the vulnerable bone covering which the germs attacked.

While these devices were being applied, the laborious grafting sessions continued. At last Johnson's entire back was covered. Dr. Browder allowed time for the final grafts to heal, then told Clifford he was ready to go to work on the other side.

The task of turning him over was given to four Coast Guard corpsmen. They were not strangers to Clifford, for everyday they came to City Hospital for the sole purpose of supplying the muscle needed to lift Clifford from his bed so that his nurses could change it. By the time he was ready to be turned, they were experts at handling him without causing damage or pain.

Clifford was absolutely delighted when his service buddies lifted him high off the bed, deftly turned him over, and lowered him down carefully into a position he had not lain in for more than six months. "Now I can see what you all are up to," he said to Dr. Browder.

Clifford's legs were so stiff that he could not move them; his elbows and armpits had webbed together and were useless. But the improvements in his morale had never been so marked. He was on his back like a normal bed patient, and he was clearly headed for recovery.

Browder then began to work on Johnson's topside. He had to cover the gaping "osteo" on his leg and patch up the hole that went down to Clifford's ribs. There were also tricky grafts to be done under his arms and on his hands. But Browder was spurred on by the beautiful back on which he had worked so long to plant six thousand separate grafts.

Clifford Johnson was Newton Browder's greatest challenge. He continually required more time, more skill, and was in more difficulty than any case Browder had encountered. The surgeon had long since fallen into the habit of bringing Johnson's problems home with him, discussing them with his wife so thoroughly that she came to know the case almost as well as a consultant.

One evening Mrs. Browder heard her husband shuffle into their apartment on Boston's Fenway. There seemed an unusually long pause between the opening of the door and the closing of it. She came out of the kitchen to greet him.

His face was dark with dejection. She had never seen him look so utterly crushed; she would not have been surprised if he had begun to cry.

"Johnson," he said. "We lost everything off his back."

He slumped into a chair and was silent for a long time. Mrs. Browder sat with him, waiting until he could bring himself to tell her.

Then he began to speak in a sad monotone. They had apparently turned Clifford over too soon. He had been restless. His twistings and turnings had taken a terrible toll. Every one of the thousands of laboriously planted grafts had shifted, pulled away, and sloughed off.

They would have to start all over again, right from the very beginning.

17

EVERYONE who worked in Boston City Hospital heard about the loss of Clifford's back, and suffered for him. When he had to be returned to the uncomfortable position in which he had lain for months, he accepted it quietly. There was nothing to indicate the degree of despondency he must have felt.

But that degree was measured by means of an attempted conspiracy which did not come to light until it no longer mattered.

Clifford sent word to Coast Guard headquarters that he would like to see Harold Davis, the buddy who had arranged the date for him the night of the Grove fire. Davis and his girl had escaped without injury. Ever since the fire, Harold had waited for permission to visit Clifford.

It was apparent to Davis as soon as he entered the hospital room that Clifford had something urgent to talk about.

Conversation was awkward and halting until they were alone.

Then Clifford said, "I want you to promise to do something for me."

Davis said he would try.

"No!" said Clifford. "I want you to promise!"

Davis had to hedge again, but he said, "I really can't promise till you tell me what it is. But if it's something I can do, I'll do it."

Clifford hesitated. Then he said it: "I want you to bring me a loaded gun."

Davis refused. He tried to encourage Clifford, but could tell that he was not being heard. He left shortly, wondering whether it would be right to betray the confidence by telling Dr. Browder what Clifford had asked him to do. His final decision was to keep the secret.

This was the only incident in Johnson's entire battle in which he revealed, even for a moment, any indication that he was not struggling to the utmost to get well. Those who knew him believe this was only a temporary lapse. Some flatly refuse to believe Davis' story. Others are sure that if Davis had brought the gun, Clifford would certainly have rejected it. Clifford was well known for fussing and grumbling, but most of it was no more serious than the good-humoured beefing that servicemen indulge in as a habit.

In fact, it was regarded as an indication of his adjustment to the loss of his back grafts when he resumed fussing. This came a few days after he'd been turned on to his stomach again. The grousing was like a sign of spring, except for one of its overtones.

He fussed continually for codeine.

The doctors and nurses had all known it was coming. Over the months codeine had provided Clifford's only respite from what might well have been the most continuous and severe pain endured by a human. He got codeine every day, and before each grafting session he got an extra dose. It was inevitable that he would become addicted.

In one attempt to prevent the drug from becoming a habit

he had been given a shot of Demerol, the sedative commonly given to women in labour. The Demerol nearly killed him. He had soared off into shock and fever. After that Dr. Browder, who had not authorized the shot, forbade anything but codeine.

So even after his pain began to slacken, Clifford demanded his dope. Mercy Smith had to listen to all manner of whining and pleading, but she would never let him have more than his chart called for.

Even this was too much, however. Dr. Browder listened to Johnson's exaggerated complaints of pain and watched the perspiration bubbling up on his face and good skin. He decided that the time for action had come.

Mercy Smith and Ellen Camper, another of Clifford's nurses, were in the room at the time. Dr. Browder asked them to leave him alone with Clifford for a while. When they went out he closed the door and locked it.

There are several techniques for withdrawing a person from narcotics. This is the one Browder used:

"Now you listen to me—and you listen good.

"Do you know what you're doing with this stuff? You're making yourself a bum—just a plain bum, and you'll be stumbling around the streets trying to scratch up enough money to stay a bum.

"If you want to do that, it's O.K. by me. But I'll tell you one thing, Sonny Boy, you're not going to be a bum on me. And you're not going to be a bum on this hospital either.

"I know when you've got pain, and I know when you haven't got it. And when you've got pain, I'll do something about it.

"But as of right this minute you're off that stuff in this hospital. You can holler and you can yowl all you want to, but you don't get any more. Do you understand me?"

"Yes, sir," said Johnson.

"All right then. This is the end of it!"

They cut him off clean.

Clifford went through private hell for the next five days. The night nurses were sure that he was not sleeping at all. He groaned, he loudly cursed the whole world, and he treated Dr. Browder with open hostility.

But everyone sensed that these were only the battle sounds of the private war Clifford was waging over his body. Drug addiction is a positive organic demand for chemicals which the body has come to require, and is as slow to heal as a wound. Clifford demonstrated every degree of his agony, but he did not once ask to be given another shot.

On the sixth morning he woke up smiling. He told Mercy Smith a long, slow story about how he used to walk through the woods in Missouri, just watching the squirrels and the birds. When Dr. Browder came in, Clifford made reference to a secret bit of information he had picked up that invariably caused exquisite embarrassment to the surgeon. Browder took the ribbing with a broad grin. He knew that Johnson had licked something which could have been just as dangerous as any of the crises he had overcome since the Cocoanut Grove fire.

About the time Clifford went off codeine, he began to avail himself of a singular form of self-prescribed therapy: girls.

He adored them, and he had a charm that brought them in gushing droves to his room. The student nurses, the aides, the young graduates—all of them made him their pet.

By then his case was so celebrated that he received a big volume of mail every day. People sent gifts, food, candy, and pictures. But if Clifford wanted to write back, it was a sure bet that the letter was to some pretty girl who had sent him a snapshot.

Mercy Smith was continually amused and amazed at his technique. She acknowledged, too, that he cut quite a figure for his guests. He had a handsome face which had healed without a noticeable scar. He had a slightly one-sided smile, beautiful teeth, and sparkling eyes. To girls long accustomed to the twang of New England speech, Clifford's slow Missouri drawl was a distinct attraction.

He never neglected a chance to flirt. Whenever a new girl appeared, Clifford would go as far as possible to line her up for some vague future engagement. He was most poised, Mercy Smith noticed, when he lay on his back, for then he could conceal a bald spot on the back of his head. He was vain about his physical appearance, and the bald spot—a result of the fire—troubled him a great deal.

Dr. Browder gradually became aware that Clifford's loss of hair was of as much concern to him as anything else he had suffered. Clifford instituted a campaign of questions about hair growth, medical advances on baldness, and the possible side benefits of all the protein concentrates he was taking.

If it had been possible to graft hair from one person to another, Johnson could have been a Sampson; every girl in the hospital would have been delighted to give him a dozen or so follicles to help restore his full head of hair.

Finally Dr. Browder could take no more.

He said to him in a hoarse stage whisper, "You want some hair up there? I can fix that for you. Now you understand it will have to be your own hair, and I'll have to take it from where it's available. So it may be black, and a little curly, but it'll be hair!"

That closed the subject permanently.

But Clifford went on to other researches. Somehow he secretly promoted the services of a toupee expert. The area to be filled was not large, and there was an abundance of hair around it. The finished hair piece combed into his own beautifully.

On the first day that he wore it, Clifford told Mercy Smith to say nothing about the toupee. When Dr. Browder came in to make his daily check, Clifford greeted him as usual. He turned his head left and right in the course of chatting with him, but Browder's concern, of course, was entirely with the grafting sites.

Finally Clifford said to him, "I wish you'd look up here on the back of my neck. I got a sore there again."

At last Browder saw the toupee. "How in the world did you do that?" he asked, amazed.

Clifford grinned. "I got connections."

The girls and the hair were only incidents in the long, steady grind of grafting and repair. With each succeeding session Dr. Browder was reducing the area through which Clifford could lose body fluids. This meant that less and less of the enormous quantity of protein that he was taking in was being lost. Instead, his body was using it to rebuild muscle and tissue. Johnson was absorbing daily more protein than is contained in ten pounds of beefsteak. Because he could now retain it, his body built up swiftly. Soon he began to show signs of the robust health which had helped carry him through his ordeal.

His health made possible an incredible concentration of surgery over the four-month period. Dr. Browder worked through twenty-one surgical sessions on the grafting alone, taking between 25,000 and 30,000 pinpoints of skin and transplanting them on to the burns. In addition, he had to figure out how to cut and graft around Clifford's elbows and shoulders where the tissues had webbed together so drastic-ally that Clifford could not move his arms at all.

The leg osteo was especially stubborn. Dr. Browder tried many methods, including a complicated technique involving shirt buttons, black silk suture, and bird shot. The idea was to pass the thread through one of the shirt buttons, anchored to the skin, then across the wound to another. The buttons held the sutures so they would not pull out under the strain. Along the sutures at various points he fastened pieces of split bird shot. Each day he would tighten the sutures a little, crimp them in place with the bird shot, and hope that everything would hold until the wound finally came together.

But it didn't. The whole thing sloughed off.

Dr. Browder tried to repair that osteo again and again. Finally he managed to get the bone covered, but he was pretty sure Clifford would continue to have trouble with infection there.

In the months after it became astoundingly clear that Clifford would recover, he came under the surveillance of a battery of doctors, nurses, chemists, technicians, specialists, and medical photographers. His case accumulated an astonishing collection of statistics.

He had received so many blood transfusions—many of them during one grave crisis or another—that inevitably some of them had not been recorded. However, the total was known to be at least sixty.

Dr. Browder also totalled the amount of blood which had been taken from him and from the transfusions just for samples to be tested in the laboratory. This amounted to about nine full pints by itself.

The day-by-day case record ran to hundreds of pages—it stacked up more than a foot high when piled on a table. Leo Goodman, who was in Browder's opinion the finest medical photographer in the country, made more than six hundred pictures of Clifford's body, most of them in colour.

These were a source of mental anguish for Clifford—he loathed being photographed. It was completely beyond his understanding that the pictures could be viewed with no judgment of him as a personality, and could prove invaluable to doctors and medical students who would see them. Every session before the cameras was, to him, total humiliation. He pleaded with Dr. Browder not to make him pose his battered body.

But Clifford Johnson's case was a classic. By staying alive he had taught his doctors more about the treatment of severe burns than had been learned from any single burn patient in the entire history of medicine.

More medical papers touched upon one or another aspect of his recovery than had ever been written about a single burn case before. It was estimated that the total cost of his treatment was $110,000, and this did not include the fees his doctors would have received if he had been a private patient.

But although Clifford was now comparatively free of pain and definitely on the mend, his struggle did not end with the completion of the grafts.

During his first six months in the hospital, Clifford had been unable to move at all. As a result, his joints had become stiff and useless. Also, the grafted skin became fantastically tough—as stiff and unyielding as a hide of tanned leather. Dr. Browder faced the problem of loosening him up without breaking any of the board-hard skin.

Mrs. Adelena Kelly, a nurse, joined Mercy Smith in the day time for the sole purpose of giving Clifford the physical therapy he had to have to unkink him. She told Dr. Browder that cocoa butter had been used successfully to soften skin, so he encouraged her to try it.

Every day Mrs. Kelly and Mercy Smith rubbed Clifford's

skin grafts with cocoa butter. They used so much that its acquisition became a problem, for the war had shortened the supply. Gradually the skin began to soften and give. Then they started to exercise him.

There is probably no greater discomfort possible than that which comes from trying to move a limb which hasn't been moved for a long time. Clifford's whole body was stiff and constricted. When Mrs. Kelly bore down on his knees, he felt the protesting stretch of tendons, ligaments, and muscle fibres. Such physical therapy is hard work for the therapist, but it's torture for the patient.

Clifford groaned, grumbled, and hollered in protest as Mrs. Kelly and Mercy worked on him. But he never once told them to stop. The two nurses would stand on opposite sides of the bed and pitch his stiff leg back and forth between them, sometimes for an hour at a stretch. They became impervious to his howls, except to notice that when he stopped complaining it meant the joints had loosened and the arc of their motion ought to be increased.

On July 28, 1943, Clifford sat up for the first time. He was as giddy as a schoolgirl as he perched on the edge of the bed. His knees were still stiff and he could only raise his arms to his shoulders, but he was delighted with his accomplishment.

In the next month his big objective was to get on to his feet. The cocoa butter massages had worked so well that on most of the burned areas Clifford could pick up the skin between two fingers. The arduous routine of exercises, massage, and repair seemed endless.

On August 31, his feet touched the floor. He put his arms around Mercy and Mrs. Kelly and, with their support, walked about eight feet to a chair.

On September 14 he walked by himself for the first time.

"Ain't that somethin'?" he said, and all the newspapers used it for a picture caption.

Through the rest of September and October, Clifford worked hard, co-operating now without complaint. It had been a long and miserable ordeal, but he could see the end of it; his big objective became to get out of the hospital before the anniversary date of the fire—November 28.

By the middle of November Clifford was walking fairly well. He practised by visiting every corner of the remarkable institution that had helped to save his life. On one of these trips he slipped on the marble floor and fell, with his weight on his left leg. The fall ripped open the stubborn osteo there, and he had to go back to bed.

But on November 26, two days before the first anniversary of the Cocoanut Grove fire, Clifford Johnson put on his dress uniform. His small toupee was expertly combed into his own hair. Mercy Smith helped him into a wheel chair, and together they started down toward the front door.

In the lobby Clifford posed for his first full-dress press picture since the fire—and insisted that Mercy pose with him.

Then he went to the Brighton Marine Hospital to convalesce. Throughout most of the next year he returned to City Hospital for more surgery by Dr. Browder.

By then Dr. Browder had distilled, from the welter of data on Clifford, what was probably the most sought-after medical lecture ever given in Boston. It was illustrated with some of the colour slides Leo Goodman had taken from the time Clifford was first examined until he got out of bed. The lecture was enormously dramatic as well as medically informative, and Browder was invited to give it before all kinds of groups.

One night he delivered it to a group of student nurses in an out-of-town hospital. Mrs. Browder went with him.

After he finished showing the scores of slides and telling of the many crises, the lights in the auditorium were turned on and Dr. Browder told the girls he had someone with him he wanted them to meet.

All through the lecture the girls had been seeing pictures of a patient with more severe burns than any human body had ever before survived.

Some showed him at the height of the oedema crisis, when his limbs were hideously swollen, his burns glistening with fluid, and his weight less than one hundred pounds.

Now Dr. Browder was asking them to look at a tall, handsome Coast Guardsman who wore a winningly charming smile.

"Girls," Dr. Browder said, "this is Clifford Johnson."

Clifford glanced amiably from one face to another—probably picking out the pretty ones. The girls looked back for a moment, then broke into thunderous applause which they kept up for more than a minute. Mrs. Browder looked around and saw that nearly all of them had tears in their eyes. She saw, too, that Clifford was eating it up.

On September 5, 1944, Clifford was honourably discharged from the United States Coast Guard. Before going home he went to see Philip Butler, then a graduated physician practising internal medicine. Together they visited Dr. Browder, Dr. Lund, Mercy Smith, and as many as they could find of the others who had helped him.

Then he went back to his home in Sumner, Missouri, and to his mother, father, sister, and twelve brothers.

The remainder of Clifford Johnson's story reaches far away from the immediate aftermath of the Cocoanut Grove fire, but it demands and deserves pursuit.

During the second year after his return home he bumped

up against an egg crate and ripped open the persistent osteo in his left leg. The injury required medical attention. Veterans Administration doctors wanted to send him to the West Coast, which was closer, but for Clifford there was only one place and one doctor—Boston City Hospital and Newton Browder.

It was like old home week when Clifford arrived. Everyone came to see him, including the new student nurses who hadn't been there when he was recovering from his burns.

One of these was a pretty Irish girl from Dorchester named Marion Donovan. She was to graduate from training that September. Marion was no more immune to Johnson's magic than any of the other girls, but her case was different: Clifford fell in love with her.

They met in April. In July he appeared on the radio show, "We, The People." Soon after, they decided to get married.

The wedding took place on September 10, 1946. Before they left for Sumner, Dr. Browder said to Marion, "I hope you've got an Irish sense of humour, because you're going to need it out there in all that Missouri mud."

"There's no such thing as mud in Missouri," Clifford said. "As soon as the rain hits the ground, somethin' nice starts to grow and soaks it all up."

Leo Goodman, the medical photographer, took a colour picture of the bride and groom before they left. It showed a handsome young man and a lovely girl, obviously in love with each other. It was a close-up, but there was no marring detail to suggest that the man had once been a black mass of burns with no real chance of survival.

The important thing to remember about Clifford Johnson from this point on is that he and his wife had ten happy years together in the farm country that he loved. These were ten years which no one ever expected would be his to live through at all. But they are years which seem to lose some of their significance when the final fact of Clifford Johnson's life is revealed. This is a fact of such bitter and outrageous irony that not one of the people who knew and loved him can bear to talk about it.

Clifford and Marion first tried running a small café. But the work and the heat were too much for his bad leg. They sold out, and he drove a cab in Kansas City. But Clifford was a country boy; before long his tolerance for avenues and boulevards dissolved. He and Marion went back to Sumner.

Sumner is called the goose capital of the world. Thousands of geese live and multiply in its huge preserve. When the government decided to open a portion of the preserve to hunting, game wardens were needed, and Clifford got one of the jobs.

He spent what was probably the happiest year of his life there. His work kept him outdoors in the woodlands and countryside he had always loved.

On December 20, 1956, Clifford was driving home from the game preserve in a jeep. There was soggy snow on the ground, and thick, rising fog above it. His jeep struck a soft shoulder, darted off the road, and overturned. He was pinned under it alive.

The sole witness to the accident could do nothing to get him out, and so went to get the only medical help available in the area—Marion Johnson.

The jeep's petrol tank had broken in the crash. Petrol soaked the entire vehicle and ran down all over Clifford. When it reached the hot block of the engine, it burst into flame.

And so Clifford Johnson died a terrible death in fire.

18

IN pursuing what became of the Cocoanut Grove's dead, dying, and injured, it has been necessary to move far forward in time from that bleak Sunday morning at the end of November when the city of Boston awoke to learn what had happened the night before.

But the damage of the fire was not confined to what happened immediately. It was to range far into the future, and to affect—directly or indirectly—people in every part of the nation.

In order to examine the fire from the point of view of those who did not hear of it until after the disaster had struck, it is necessary to return to that Sunday morning.

Close to five hundred people were dead. The hospitals were filled with victims. Almost everyone in Boston—and that included thirty cities and towns around it—claimed to know someone who had been at the Grove on Saturday night.

Fire Commissioner William Arthur Reilly began his investigation on Sunday morning. It was his responsibility to determine not only the cause and nature of the fire, but whether the Fire Department had fulfilled its duties in inspecting the Grove for fire safety before it burned.

A second probe, to establish who was to blame for the

catastrophe, was started the following day. Reilly's probe was open to the press and the public, but the other, conducted jointly by the Massachusetts attorney general and the Boston district attorney, was held in private.

The district attorney, William J. Foley, in announcing that he and the attorney general would investigate jointly, issued a blast at widespread laxity, and announced that findings would be presented to a grand jury as early as possible.

Attorney General Robert T. Bushnell authorized Fire Marshal Stephen J. Garrity to probe into all aspects of the fire, the building code, fire inspection, wiring, and licences. Garrity, who was to receive daily transcripts of testimony heard by Reilly, told newsmen that he intended to follow the evidence wherever it led, no matter whom it hurt.

James H. Mooney, the building commissioner, told another press gathering that the whole structure of laws governing restaurants and night clubs was, and had long been, in need of complete revamping. He said there was nothing in the law to prevent the use of inflammable decorations, or to require well-marked exits, in such places. The only stipulation was that there be two exits, which the Cocoanut Grove had.

Mooney said further that his department was empowered to order the spraying of theatre interiors and decorations with fireproofing materials, but couldn't do anything to see that night clubs took the same precautions.

"I want a law to prohibit the use of inflammables for decorative purposes," he concluded. "Sprinklers would have reduced the death toll appreciably, but restaurants are not required to have them."

As a one-storey structure, the main building of the Grove was also exempt from the stiff fire laws governing taller buildings. This prompted Robert S. Moulton, technical secretary of the National Fire Protective Association, to issue a statement on Monday that local building laws were "chaotic."

The Licensing Board reacted to the disaster by issuing a blanket order forbidding restaurants that featured entertainment or dancing from opening until they were inspected. Enforcing this order, the Police Department closed every establishment thus described—plus all cafés, taverns, lounges, and bars of other description—until further notice.

A precious horse had been stolen. Everyone wanted to be the first to lock the barns.

The first witnesses to testify before the fire commissioner were Fire Department officers, most of whom had repeatedly offered up their lives in the course of evacuating victims from the burning Grove.

But the eleventh witness was Lieutenant Frank J. Linney, of the Fire Prevention Division. On November 20—eight days before the fire—he had made an official fire-prevention inspection of the Cocoanut Grove. As Linney sat in the witness chair waiting to testify, Commissioner Reilly studied the report the officer had turned in:

City of Boston

FIRE DEPARTMENT

Fire Prevention Division

60 Bristol Street

William Arthur Reilly
Fire Commissioner

John J. Kenney
Deputy Chief

November 30, 1942

FROM: The Fire Prevention Division

TO: The Fire Commissioner

SUBJECT: Inspection, Cocoanut Grove, 17 Piedmont Street.

OWNER AND MGR.: Barnet Wilansky, Night Club.
Building: 1 storey, occupies approximately 7,500 square feet.

I submit the following report of inspection made this day, November 20, 1942 and in my opinion condition of the premises is good.

A new addition has been added on the Broadway side used as a cocktail lounge room, seating 100 people. No inflammable decoration.

Main dining room seating 400 people.

Old tenement houses next to new lounge room.

2nd floor used as dressing room.

3rd floor used as help locker room.

This building connects into hallway between lounge and main dining room.

Kitchen in basement, free from grease, hood over stove, underside, clean. Cocktail bar.

Sufficient number of exits.

Sufficient number of extinguishers.

Heat, using fuel oil, 2-275 gallon tank and coal.

Condition—Good.

> Respectfully submitted
> (Signed) FRANK J. LINNEY
> Lieutenant.

Even without a Cocoanut Grove fire, the report would almost have been a classic of its kind. It was the type of document with which every department of government is plagued: a report required by law to be filed with hundreds of others like it, it contained information which most likely would never be seen, and was couched in an economy of language that stripped it of meaning; furthermore, it was riddled with errors. It even began with a colossal mistake—

the wrong date, November 30. This was explained as a typographical error, but it set the mood in which the remainder of the document was examined.

The name of the owner, Barnet Welansky, was mis-spelled.

There were probably two hundred people seated in the New Lounge. Linney's report specified one hundred seats.

There were six hundred or more in the Main Dining Room. Linney's report specified four hundred.

The only reference to the Melody Lounge and its flagrantly combustible decorations was in the verbless sentence, "Cocktail Bar."

Reilly read the entire report aloud. Then he and Chief of Department Pope began questioning Linney.

The witness testified that he had touched a match to the leaves and wrappings of the palm trees, the blue satin, the leatherette, the bamboo, the rattan, and the netting. Nothing had burned, he said.

Reilly pressed him for precise detail as to whether the materials blackened or crinkled when the match was applied, and asked how long he had held each material in the flame.

Lieutenant Linney answered the questions forthrightly, insisting he had done everything department policy required him to do.

He sat motionless in the witness chair as Reilly scanned the report again. The room was completely silent.

Then Reilly asked, "Do you still feel, in the light of what happened, that the condition of the Cocoanut Grove was 'good' on November twentieth?"

"Positively!" said Linney.

"There was nothing to lead you to believe that a small fire breaking out there would spread as it did?"

"No. If I had they'd have got a notice."

From that moment it was clear that Linney was to be one of the scapegoats. The reporters present had to acknowledge that Linney testified bravely and with apparent sincerity. But the errors in the report, the scanty information, and the final description of the Grove's condition as "good" condemned him in the public's eye.

Dr. Charles F. Brooks, director of Harvard University's weather station on Milton's Big Blue Hill, gave testimony that could have helped Linney but did not. His records showed that November 20, the day Linney had made his inspection, was the wettest day of the month. The high humidity, Brooks said, plus the fact that Linney made his tests in the unfinished New Lounge where workmen were continually lettting in outside air, might have prevented many combustible materials from igniting in a match flame.

"If Lieutenant Linney had examined on another day, he might have found that materials which would not burn on November twentieth were inflammable," Dr. Brooks said.

Laboratory tests substantiated Brooks' claim. Grove materials tested on December 2, a very damp day, did not burn as rapidly as those tested the following day, when the humidity was lower. Brooks' best estimate, based on his records, was that the relative humidity in the Grove on the night of the fire could not have been higher than twelve per cent. This figure, he said, forestry officials had long regarded as evidence that an extreme fire hazard existed.

With no intention to hurt Linney further, Brooks criticized the policy of fire inspection because it did not take relative humidity into account. He offered the information constructively, but it was all that most Bostonians needed to make their condemnation of Linney complete.

Barney Welansky was still in the hospital during the

opening days of Reilly's hearings. His brother, Jimmy, took his place on the stand. Jimmy had no official connection with the Grove, except that he had been acting as manager on the night the fire occurred. But Jimmy's earlier life, as well as Barney's, came under the scrutiny of the public as newspapers published "sidebar" stories informing their readers of the past actions of those associated with the Grove.

It was brought to light that a report on the murder of David J. "Beano" Breen, which took place in 1938, had involved Jimmy Welansky, who at that time was managing the Theatrical Club and the Metropolitan Hotel. Evidence from the murder investigation revealed that Breen and Welansky were engaged in a gaming enterprise at a recreation centre called Nantasket Beach. The enterprise failed, leaving Welansky to absorb by himself a $20,000 loss. Though Breen's murder followed soon after, Welansky was cleared of any connection with the crime. But his mere association with a murdered gambler was enough to suggest to Boston newspaper readers that his character was questionable, and that part of the blame for the tragedy was his.

Jimmy's testimony did not help the reputation of his brother. When Reilly asked about fire inspection at the Grove, or the flameproofing of decorations, or the policy of locking certain doors at certain times, Jimmy replied, "I don't know." Though this was an honest answer, it sounded evasive. Many people assumed that Jimmy's ignorance of Grove policy was feigned in an effort to avoid prosecution and to protect his brother.

Barney's own past did little to improve the general impression. It was made public that pictures and fingerprints of one Barnet Welansky had been on file at Boston Police Headquarters, but had been removed on the direct order of the police commissioner. The explanation offered by the police was that Welansky's folder had simply been taken out of the file reserved for known criminals and placed in an "inactive file." But when it was demanded that the record be produced, no such Welansky folder could be found.

This revelation was quickly associated with another apparent tie-up between the Welanskys and the Police Department. Jimmy Welansky, when asked how he happened to have escaped from the burning Grove, testified that he had been swept out of the Lounge with Buccigross, the police captain.

The image of a night-club manager and a police captain successfully escaping from a building in which hundreds had died was one that set already angry imaginations afire.

When it came his turn, Buccigross went to the witness stand a bewildered, humiliated man. In the four days since the fire, he had learned that he was almost universally resented for having been in the Grove in the first place, for having been out of uniform—and, it seemed, for not having died.

Buccigross told his story. It was closely corroborated by the testimony Welansky had already given, and by Garrett H. Byrne, the assistant district attorney, with whom had sat in the New Lounge.

But these were stories nobody wanted to believe. Buccigross was a cop. He had escaped. Nearly five hundred had not.

The tales about Buccigross ballooned swiftly. He was said to have gone to the Grove "to get paid off." He was described as "roaring drunk." Rumours were circulated as to how he "knocked down women to get out."

But "Spider" Murphy, who had been with Buccigross, and who had no reason to be other than impartial, knew that these stories were not true. He did not take the stand to testify—but, even if he had, it is doubtful that his story would have helped Buccigross any more than Byrne's did.

Police Commissioner Joseph F. Timilty, wearing the double-breasted, velvet-collared Chesterfield and pearl-grey Homburg by which Boston politicians identified themselves, defended Buccigross, testifying that the police captain had every right and duty to be present in the Cocoanut Grove. In fact, he said, he would consider Buccigross remiss in his duties if he did not appear there regularly.

Timilty also said that he would prefer that Buccigross make such inspections in civilian clothes rather than in uniform, as this would enable him more readily to spot gambling, serving to minors and drunks, and solicitation by women.

Superintendent Fallon followed Timilty to the stand, substantially repeating the commissioner's testimony. Unfortunately for Buccigross, however, Fallon added one duty to those which an officer might perform while inspecting a place like the Grove: "Breaking up overcrowding."

This, Buccigross clearly had not done. Nor could he have done so had he tried. Barney Welansky's connections with City Hall were obviously such that it would have been foolish for the night captain of the South End police division to have ordered him to send patrons home. One telephone call to the "right" person, and Buccigross might have found himself tending City Prison or filing fingerprints in the Bureau of Criminal Investigation. As second in command to the day captain of the police division, Buccigross believed that any blame for the overcrowding of the Grove should be placed, not upon him, but upon his superior, with whom he assumed Welansky had made "arrangements."

But Buccigross' testimony was interpreted in an atmosphere of hostility created by the anguished accounts of several victims who had preceded him to the stand. Public bitterness had also been increased when it was learned that the entire tragedy had resulted from what would have been an insignificant episode in a bar, had the patrons of the Grove been properly protected against fire.

For Maurice Levy had also told his story on the witness stand.

Jean, his bride of only eight months, had died at Cambridge City Hospital. Reilly had hoped it would not be necessary to call as witness anyone who had suffered an intimate loss in the fire, but as accounts of Levy's experience reached him, he realized that the young widower's story was too important not to be heard.

Reilly had apologized to Levy, and asked him to recount what he had seen. Levy testified quietly, without rancour. He described every detail, from the manner in which the Melody Lounge patron had unscrewed the light bulb in the cocoanut husk, to the fact that the bar boy had disposed of the match with care.

The story made sense. There could be no doubt that this was what had happened in the darkened corner of the Melody Lounge.

19

A S Reilly's investigation continued, a significant discrepancy began to emerge. Virtually every patron who testified insisted that the Grove had been badly overcrowded. But the employees of the Grove, almost to a man, asserted that nothing was unusual about the number of patrons accommodated that night.

This was a crucial point, and Reilly knew that it should be developed. But it would have to be developed at the attorney general's hearings, not at Reilly's—for the fire commissioner's primary concern was to establish that his men had saved as many lives as possible and had shown no lack of courage.

No one yet had any accurate idea as to how many patrons and employees had actually occupied the club when the fire broke out. But patrons who took the stand used such expressions as "wickedly overcrowded" and "jammed to the doors." If this were truly the case, then the fire fighters were to be credited with a magnificent accomplishment for having saved as many lives as they did.

Reilly learned of certain areas in the Main Dining Room where extra tables could be set up to accommodate patrons on busy nights. The extra tables were not set up all at once, but were brought in gradually as additional patrons arrived. Only when all these tables were occupied would Balzerini, the headwaiter, begin to turn newcomers away.

Subsequent testimony established that, on the night of the fire, Balzerini had had to set up the extra tables at an unusually early hour. Much of the crowd consisted of people who did not ordinarily frequent night clubs but had reserved tables at the Grove in anticipation of a B.C. victory celebration. They came in such numbers that, by nine o'clock, Balzerini had already given the order to begin turning customers away. But so many patrons arrived during the next hour, all insisting they would not object to sitting "anywhere at all," that Balzerini finally decided to set up additional tables on the dance floor itself!

When, on the basis of the number of these extra tables, it was estimated that between 900 and 1,000 patrons had been packed into a night club whose licence allowed for only 460, the demand increased that Barney Welansky be brought to justice.

But Barney was still a patient in Massachusetts General Hospital, and could not be forced to testify. After being discharged from the hospital by his doctor, Harry B. Levine, he was ordered home to bed. Levine signed an affidavit saying that his patient was too ill to appear at the investigation.

Public sentiment seethed against Barney. He was vilified in letters published by Massachusetts newspapers. One anonymous letter-writer threatened Dr. Levine's life if he did not permit his patient to "face up to what he has coming."

Two sensational developments made matters worse for Welansky.

Firemen, who had returned to the Grove to search for persons still missing, stumbled on to a huge storage vault behind the rear wall of the Melody Lounge. In the vault were 4,100 cases of liquor—whisky, wine, beer, and champagne—that were untouched by fire and unaffected by heat. The Federal Bureau of Internal Revenue quickly proved that a large tax due on the liquor was unpaid, and won a court attachment on the entire cache.

It was also discovered that the Grove account books, rescued from the fire, were missing. The Fire Department had turned them over to South End police on the night of the disaster. On someone's authority—it was never determined whose—the books were then released by the Police to representatives of Herbert Callahan, Barney Welansky's law partner. By the time investigators learned of the existence of the books and ordered their return, it was feared they had been altered.

The financial status of the Grove, as revealed by the account books, added fuel to the fire of public indignation. The court appointed a receiver of Grove assets, who collected $171,000 from the sale of liquor in the vaults and $80,000 on insurance policies held by Welansky. Except for a small cash account in the local bank, this was the total amount available to settle the hundreds of claims that already had been filed by victims or their families. Divided by seven hundred, the approximate number of victims, it would have provided less than $360 for each.

But even this small sum began to shrink. The court-appointed receiver spent $20,000 in the process of collecting the assets. Another $50,000 was earmarked for Grove creditors. The Federal Government claimed $100,000 as tax on the liquor. Less than $85,000 remained. Even when creditors, who had little hope of collecting anyway, agreed to forego payment in order to make larger death and injury awards available, it was clear that nobody was likely to receive settlement commensurate with his suffering.

The financial report, the stories coming out of hospitals, the accounts of tax evasion, kept public pressure high—although it was Reilly's probe, open to reporters, that provided most of the copy for newspapers. But there were certain aspects of the case which were not Reilly's to pursue. Accordingly, he tried to restrict the testimony of witnesses to details of the fire. Any statement suggestive of violation of statutes, felonious intent, or actual crime he assiduously refused to examine, cautioning the witnesses that such matters must be reserved for the public prosecutor.

This he saw as his duty. According to Massachusetts law in 1942, the fire commissioner served only as the public's representative in the Fire Department. He did not administer the department's affairs in the same way, say, as a police commissioner, nor was he empowered to enforce fire-prevention measures, which existed merely as "policy." Reilly was responsible only for the investigation of fires and the efficiency of the department in putting them out and rescuing victims.

Nonetheless, his investigation seemed to uncover startling information with virtually every witness. Bank auditors, fire-alarm experts, chemists, insurance executives, all gave evidence that the Grove met only the minimum requirements of the law.

Yet the only record of official disciplinary action against the Grove was an order dated November 19, 1937, requiring the management to desist from referring to the place as a "night club" in its advertisements. Night clubs, as such, were illegal in Boston. Though the Cocoanut Grove supplied every requisite of night club atmosphere, it was licensed as a "restaurant," and therefore could not call itself anything else.

One of the documents entered as evidence was the Grove's application for a new licence, on which the seating capacity for the entire Grove had been listed as "four hundred and sixty." This was a shocking figure to a citizenry that knew there were already more than 460 dead, to say nothing of nearly 200 victims suffering in hospitals. The application also sought approval of thirty additional fixed stools for the New Lounge. Though permission had not yet been granted, these stools had already been installed, on the assumption that the Licensing Board would raise no objection.

Louis Epple, a member of the Licensing Board, testified that the Grove had obtained its original licence and several renewals without any hearings as to whether it complied with regulations.

Epple's testimony suggested to investigators that they should explore the relationship between the Grove and the Building Department. Building Commissioner Mooney, who had risked his life in an effort to roll back the sliding roof, testified that, technically, the Grove had exits sufficient for the escape of thirteen hundred people. His inspector, Theodore Eldracher, showed by the use of a diagram that the Grove had more than enough exits to comply with the antiquated law, although few patrons had been able to pass through them.

The weakness in the law, both pointed out, was that one doorway could be regarded as an "exit" for both of the rooms it connected. Fire safety regulations enabled each of the entertainment rooms in the Cocoanut Grove to be considered as separate and independent areas. So long as a fire was confined to any one of them, there were enough doors to get patrons either safely to the street or into another room. The law did not take into account the possibility of fire raging from one room to another before patrons could escape through the doors provided.

For example, the doorway from the kitchen to the Melody Lounge fulfilled the requirements of an exit for each, on the theory that a fire would be in one room or the other, but not both.

The locked panic door, of course, was in flagrant violation of the law. But even if it had been operating it was not large enough to protect patrons against fires breaking out in both the Melody Lounge and the Foyer. The fire and safety regulations, despite their intent, were completely inadequate to the structure of the Cocoanut Grove, Eldracher and Mooney agreed.

Eldracher was asked if any inspection had been made of the Grove during the period in which the New Lounge was under construction. He said that he himself had visited the Grove and found that the only construction error was the absence of a steel-covered fire door between the New Lounge and the Main Dining Room. This had been purchased, he said, but because of the wartime steel shortage, had not been delivered.

He admitted, however, that the New Lounge had been allowed to open even though the Building Department had never issued a certificate of inspection.

When Eldracher was questioned about the wiring in the New Lounge, he said that such information would have to be given by the wiring inspector, Frank H. Kelly, who was called to the stand.

Kelly testified that although the new electrical work in the Cocoanut Grove met the requirements of the law, the management had never applied for a wiring permit. Moreover, the work had not been done by a master electrician, thus violating another provision in the law.

Two notices of violation had been sent out by the department, Kelly said, and a third had been about to follow. If the third had been ignored, the department would have removed the Grove's meter and shut off the power.

Intrigued by the apparent flagrancy of the wiring violation the probers called Raymond Baer, of Brighton, who had installed the wiring for the New Lounge. Baer confirmed that he was not a master electrician. But he said he had been told that the management would "take care" of obtaining a permit for the work and inspecting it when it was done.

Then Henry Weene took the stand.

Weene operated a neon-sign business in the Charlestown section of Boston. Because the neon signs and lights in the Grove required a special power apparatus that was known to generate heat, Weene was questioned as to whether the device had been installed in compliance with the law.

Weene showed himself to be very much on the defensive from the moment he was sworn in. In the midst of a fairly innocuous line of questioning on the nature of the neon apparatus he suddenly blurted out, "I'm not going to be left holding the bag!"

Commissioner Reilly asked him what he meant.

Weene said, "When I was called in by Welansky in October, and he told me about what he wanted in the New Lounge, I said to him, 'This job calls for a permit.' I told him either he or I could arrange for a master electrician to do the wiring work. Welansky told me that wouldn't be necessary."

Then he added, "Welansky said to me, 'You won't have to get a permit because Tobin and I fit. They owe me plenty down there.'"

Reilly responded quickly. "Now, Mr. Weene, are you sure

those were the words used by Mr. Welansky? The exact words?"

"I am positive!"

Mayor Maurice Tobin immediately issued a stinging denial. "I want the people of Boston to know that since I have held the office of mayor, I have never, wittingly or unwittingly, permitted any winking at the law, or any violation of the law."

Furthermore, Tobin said, if Welansky had made the statement to which Weene testified, he had made it without basis. "Mr. Welansky has no right to assume his relations with City Hall are such as to permit scoffing at any aspect of the law," Tobin declared.

But the same newspapers which carried the mayor's denial also pointed out that Tobin had recently appointed Welansky to serve as a member of the city rationing board.

Reilly's probe, which had begun with the statement that everything would be open to the public no matter who was hurt, closed with an apologetic pronouncement by the city attorney. It was his legal opinion, he said, that perhaps the fire commissioner had no right to reveal testimony to the public through the press. The mayor had been advised, he continued, of "legal precedent that the hearings should be held privately."

Another reason given for the exclusion of the press from the later hearings was that Reilly intended to begin the questioning of injured Grove victims in their homes, and could not ask such victims to play host to a corps of reporters.

So the open hearings ended, but not before the public got some idea of the relationship between the Cocoanut Grove and City Hall.

A clear summary of the general policy under which the

Women volunteers played a heroic part in identifying the dead. The women above, at City Hospital, talked to relatives and morgue workers, gathering clues to identity so that few survivors had to witness the macabre scene at Southern Mortuary. (*Photo by courtesy of the Boston Globe*)

(*Below*) Friends and next-of-kin wait in the morgue's amphitheatre for word of the lost ones they seek. (*Wide World photo*)

Doctors, nurses, and interns at City Hospital hover over a victim of the fire. In the foreground are bottles of plasma, mainstay in the treatment for prevention of shock following burns. (*Photo by courtesy of the Boston Globe*)

Grove had been managed had emerged from the testimony: save as much money as possible, use political influence when necessary, and pack in patrons wherever there is room.

Boston citizens, as well as people throughout the nation, became incensed at the aura of corruption that seemed responsible for the death and injury of so many victims. Editorials urged swift justice, although they were quick to point out that true justice could never be achieved.

At headquarters of the Massachusetts Department of Public Safety, Attorney General Bushnell and District Attorney Foley had received daily transcripts of all testimony given before Reilly. The pushed their own investigation forward accordingly, carefully preparing evidence to be presented to the grand jury.

Bushnell and Foley called many of the witnesses who had appeared before Reilly. They also called witnesses who had no direct connection with the fire, but who might supply them with evidence that corruption was responsible for the conditions that had prevailed when the Grove burned.

The city censor was called to report on whether any degree of smut had been tolerated in the Grove floor show. It had not, he said; Welansky himself had often ruled out off-colour material. A police officer was asked if the Grove had observed the closing curfew regulations. It had, he stated. But because the hearings were closed, these two minor points in the Grove's favour did not reach the public.

On December 7, Boston's City Council began the screening of twenty-three grand jurors to hear the evidence obtained by Bushnell and Foley. Each prospective juror was questioned closely on whether he was related to, acquainted with, or compensated financially by anyone who died or was injured in the Cocoanut Grove.

Because this grand jury would be compelled by law to disband at the end of the calendar year, twenty-four days hence, the closed investigation pushed ahead relentlessly. The attorney general and district attorney called witnesses without respite, sometimes holding hearings in the evenings and on Saturdays.

The bulk of their case against the Grove and its management was assembled by Frederick T. Doyle, an assistant district attorney, one of the best courtroom prosecutors the city of Boston ever had.

As the month drew to a close, it began to look as though Doyle would not have enough time to finish his presentation of evidence to the jurors. In an effort to ensure that all the work done thus far had not been wasted, key witnesses were sometimes hustled directly from Public Safety Department headquarters to the Suffolk County Courtroom to repeat their testimony before the grand jury.

On December 29 the work was finished. The grand jury issued a statement charging members of various city departments who were concerned with public safety of "laxity, incompetence, failure to fulfill prescribed duties effectively and lack of complete knowledge of duties."

It was a powerful accusation and every Boston newspaper printed its text.

But the grand jury did not bow out with just a statement. Before it disbanded it handed down ten secret indictments of the people it held responsible for the disaster.

20

G RAND jury indictments following disasters are often no more than inconsequential by-products of public pressure. In Boston, for example, there had been indictments of officials following deaths resulting from the collapse of the floor in a place called the Pickwick Club, on July 4, 1925, but none of the cases had gone to trial. The *Morro Castle* tragedy of September, 1934, produced much public clamour, but no jail sentences for those involved.

Attorney General Bushnell and Assistant District Attorney Doyle determined to make the Cocoanut Grove indictments achieve results in court, and so searched the law for precedent and form.

The first indictments they obtained charged manslaughter against the Welanskys and Jack Goldfine, the wine steward whose attempts to uncouple the cables of the revolving door had been so ineffectual.

The three were charged with the specific manslaughter of John Bauer, Gina Teresa Caradonna, William Langhammer, John Murray, Jean Levy, John Donovan, Anna Stern, Adele Dreyfus, Priscilla White, Alice Murray, Josephine Donovan, Harold Ford, Elisha W. Cobb, Eleanor Chiampa, and Madeline Wennerstrand.

This was a cross section of victims representing every stratum of society, all rooms in the club, both sexes, as well as military servicemen. It thus anticipated every possible attitude in the prospective jurors.

For insurance, a set of conspiracy indictments was prepared against the three in case they won acquittal on the first trial. Doyle used the legal device of naming sixteen fictitious persons, such as John Doe, Jane Doe, Richard Roe, Helen Roe. He could thus substitute the names of actual victims later, basing his choice on information yet to be uncovered.

The seven other defendants were indicted on lesser charges. Fire Lieutenant Frank Linney was charged with neglect of duties in an indictment which said he had "omitted, neglected, and refused to perform duties as a public officer in the inspection of the Cocoanut Grove."

Police Captain Buccigross, it was charged, "Wilfully and corruptly failed, neglected, refused, and omitted to enforce the laws of the Commonwealth requiring the remedying of any conditions in or about the Cocoanut Grove in respect to fires, prevention of fires and fire hazards."

Theodore Eldracher, the building inspector, was charged with failure to report an insufficient number of exits. A separate indictment charged him with conspiring to violate the building code.

Eldracher's superior, Commissioner James H. Mooney, was shocked and bewildered to find himself a defendant. An indictment against him alleged that he had failed to enforce a law prohibiting the use of a place of public assembly until a certificate had been issued by a Building Department inspector.

Another unexpected indictment charged Reuben Bodenhorn, the famous night-club architect who had drawn the plans for the Grove, with conspiring to violate the building laws. Two of his co-conspirators, other indictments alleged, were Samuel Rudnick, the contractor who had done the work in the Grove, and David Gilbert, Rudnick's foreman.

These were the ten men chosen to bear the blame.

A second count against the police captain charged that he failed to enforce a law on removal of obstacles that might interfere with means of exit or operation of the Fire Department.

Buccigross was not seriously disturbed by the indictments. He had been expecting them since the first day of the investigation; he was confident that, when the hysteria subsided, an intelligent appraisal of his role in the fire would clear his name.

But he was stunned by what happened next. Superintendent Fallon, with whom Buccigross had begun his career as a police officer, and whom Buccigross had regarded as a close friend, suddenly suspended him from duty without pay. Fallon contended that any officer indicted for a felony must be so suspended, but Buccigross interpreted the move as "a stab in the back."

He remembered Fallon's first words to him at the fire: "Captain, go to your station and get into proper uniform." Even then, it now appeared to Buccigross, Fallon had anticipated that it might be necessary to throw Buccigross to the wolves in order to make himself look better to the public.

Bail on the manslaughter indictments was set at $10,000 for each of the three chief defendants. Lieutenant Linney and Samuel Rudnick were required to post $5,000 each for their freedom. All of the others except Eldracher were freed on $2,500. Eldracher was released on $1,000.

While he was still under indictment for manslaughter, more bad news arrived for Barney Welansky. The Federal

Government had gone over his books and charged him and his brother with income tax evasion. He was indicted by the government on March 3, and required to post another $5,000 bail.

On March 15, the ailing Barney, his brother, and the wine steward went to trial. The testimony for the most part was a repetition of what had come out during the investigation.

Two of the witnesses were chorus girls Pepper Russell and Jackie Maver, both fond of Barney, and both sure he had not committed wilfully the crimes of which he was accused. The only two Grove entertainers who had remained in Boston, they were required to testify against their former boss. As each left the stand, Barney gave a quick nod from the defendant's box, as though saying he understood.

The strongest testimony in the State's case came from Henry Weene, the neon-lighting expert. Herbert Callahan, regarded as the most devastating cross-examiner in the state, was defending the Welanskys. After Weene again quoted Welansky as saying, "Tobin and I fit," Callahan cross-examined the witness for more than two hours.

Over and over again Callahan made him tell every aspect of the incident. Weene was confronted with the testimony of Raymond Baer, the electrician, who had said he was present for the conversation and couldn't recall any such statement about the mayor. But Weene could not be shaken.

The trial dragged on. Witness after witness was called. Sessions began a half hour earlier and ended a half hour later than usual. Half-day sessions were held on Saturday, ordinarily not a court day.

Finally, on April 11, the jury was sent out to deliberate. They came back after only four hours and fifty minutes.

Jimmy Welansky and Jack Goldfine were acquitted on every count.

But as the judge read each separate count in the indictment against Barney, Joseph S. Murray, the foreman of the jury, answered "Guilty."

There were nineteen counts in the indictments. Barney was found guilty on each.

Four days later, on April 15, Barney was brought back to the courtroom. Judge Joseph L. Hurley ordered him to stand and asked if he had anything to say before hearing sentence. Barney was silent.

Then Judge Hurley said: "The Court sentences you on each count to not less than twelve nor more than fifteen years in the State Prison, to be served concurrently, the first twenty-four hours to be spent in solitary confinement and the residue at hard labour."

Barney lowered his head, and was led out of the courtroom. He was sent across the river to the Charlestown State Prison, about three miles away from the site of the Cocoanut Grove.

The second trial got under way in June, 1943. Jimmy Welansky, Eldracher, Rudnick, Gilbert, and Bodenhorn faced the charge of conspiracy to violate the building laws. After nineteen days of testimony the judge declared a mistrial without making his reason public.

The case was tried again in July. Four days before it went to the jury, the judge directed a verdict of acquittal for Bodenhorn, the architect. The jury also acquitted Welansky, Gilbert, and Eldracher, but found Rudnick guilty.

Since the charge had been conspiracy, and Rudnick alone had been found guilty, his lawyer jumped up to protest that there was nobody left with whom he could have conspired.

Accordingly, when it came time to sentence Rudnick, the judge imposed a two-year prison term, but granted a stay of its execution until the case had been appealed.

Fire Lieutenant Linney went on trial alone early in November, nearly a year after he had made the inspection of the Grove and pronounced its condition "good." He was acquitted of the charge of wilful neglect, but the experience left its mark upon him. His health failed consistently, and he died several years later.

Much of the angry passion aroused by the fire had by then subsided, and it became clear that Mooney, the building commissioner, had in no way been lax in the enforcement of building laws as they applied to the Grove. Attorney Bushnell himself arranged that the charges against Mooney be dropped.

By January of 1944, the only one of the ten still awaiting trial was the police captain, Buccigross. A year had passed in which he had received no pay and performed no duties for the Police Department. He had mortgaged his home and borrowed as much as he could. He was determined, however, to retain his status as a police officer until he could clear himself in court.

In the same month, Attorney Callahan made a plea that Barney Welansky's sentence be shortened. He told the court that Barney had overworked himself on his job as sewing-machine operator in the Charlestown State Prison, and that his health had failed as a result. Even prison officials had to acknowledge this, Callahan contended, for—five months after he had arrived at Charlestown—Barney had been transferred to the Norfolk Prison Colony where he could perform lighter work.

The court refused to shorten Welansky's twelve-to-fifteen-year sentence.

The only other one of the ten who was convicted, Rudnick, was still free on a stay of execution. When his trial was reviewed by a higher court it found that no judicial error had occurred in the first trial, and he was hence guilty as the jury had found. But because all of his alleged co-conspirators had been acquitted, the court recommended that the two-year sentence be suspended indefinitely. Rudnick never went to prison.

No further court action involving Cocoanut Grove defendants took place until July of 1944. Then the attorney general went before the Supreme Judicial Court on behalf of Buccigross, who was then in his nineteenth month of suspension without pay. Bushnell told the court that Buccigross possessed no technical knowledge of the Grove, nor had he received specific instructions concerning its patrons.

"The Cocoanut Grove was openly permitted without interference on the part of officials higher in authority than this defendant to 'pack 'em in,'" Bushnell said. "I ask that the case against this man be nol-prossed." The court agreed and the charge against Buccigross was dropped.

Buccigross was permitted to return to duty, but he lost his command. He was assigned to Police Headquarters, where he worked in daily contact with Superintendent Fallon, whom he never forgave for having suspended him. Ultimately the state legislature passed a private bill which awarded Buccigross all of his back pay. He outlived Fallon, and, when he reached retirement age, won a disability pension for injuries sustained while performing his duty at the Cocoanut Grove fire.

But the shadow of guilt was never truly removed from him in the minds of many who had been involved in the fire. Buccigross came to accept such suspicion much as those who had been badly burned accepted their scars. At least, he consoled himself, he had come out of the Grove alive.

The income tax charge against the Welanskys was not tried in Federal Court until February 21, 1945. The trial was brief. Barney and his brother were given suspended sentences for the evasion of $70,000 in income tax, part of which was represented by the sum of $130 weekly that Barney had paid to himself in the name of Mickey Alpert.

Barney's disgrace was now complete. In a gesture that was almost entirely superfluous, he had been formally disbarred by the Massachusetts Bar Association and removed from the rolls of lawyers entitled to serve as bail commissioners.

By 1946 it became apparent that he was seriously ill. Examination revealed that he had inoperable cancer. In February of that year another appeal was denied; no opinion accompanied the denial.

Barney continued to fail rapidly in health. By September of 1946 his condition was so critical as to warrant massive radiation treatment at Massachusetts General Hospital, where research in X-ray treatment of cancer was then being undertaken.

So Barney, under guard, was sent back to Phillips House, the hospital building in which he had been sleeping when fire struck the Cocoanut Grove. His lawyers made still another appeal, this time to Maurice Tobin, who had become governor. But Tobin's previous association with Barney made it imperative that he be scrupulously unbiased in any such consideration.

Tobin decided to base his decision on the opinion of the doctors who were studying Barney's case. They confirmed that Barney had fatal cancer, but said that death was not immediately imminent, and might be further forestalled by the X-ray therapy. Tobin turned down Barney's appeal.

But at the end of the month it became apparent that Barney did not have much more time. A final appeal was entered, this time through the parole board, which had the right to grant a full pardon in cases of unusual merit. The board ruled that no such pardon seemed warranted unless public hearings of those involved in the fire showed no disfavour.

Callahan, in what was now the last possible effort, managed to win a public hearing on whether Grove victims would allow his client to come out of prison to die. At the hearing Lawrence Nadeau, of Charlestown, brother of Claudia Nadeau O'Neill, who had died in the Grove with her husband on her wedding night, appealed for clemency for Barney. He told the parole board that he and his family did not believe Welansky could be held responsible for the death of his sister and the others who died with her in the Cocoanut Grove.

But Mrs. Pauline Sneider, sister of another Grove victim, demonstrated bitter resentment at the prospect that Barney might be freed. She said she intended to ask District Attorney Foley to re-open the case and seek indictments against other city officials who, she asserted, had "gotten away with murder." She urged the board to grant no leniency whatever to Welansky, not even his status as a clinical patient in Massachusetts General's cancer research project.

"Welansky should die like a rat in jail!" she shrieked.

After the public hearing, the appeal was put to the governor's Council, which voted to set Barney free. On November 7, 1946, after he had served three years and seven months, Barney Welansky came out of prison.

The Cocoanut Grove, by then, had been bulldozed into

the ground. Its rubble had been carted away and a new building, entirely unrelated to the night-club business, had been erected. No place of entertainment anywhere in Boston, the Licensing Board had ruled, could ever again call itself the Cocoanut Grove. The name was a memory the city wanted to forget.

Barney Welansky, of course, could never forget. He was fifty years old when he came out of prison, but he wore far greater age on his face. Broken, disgraced, and riddled with cancer, he had only four more months to live.

Reporters and photographers met him as he walked out of the prison yard. He was asked if he had anything to say.

"Yes," he answered in a low voice. "I wish I had died there with the others."

21

ENTIRELY apart from its terrible death toll, the Cocoanut Grove fire was a fantastic occurrence. Even if the fire had struck while the club was empty, it would have posed the same mystery : why did it burn so fast ?

The point of origin of the fire was of no real significance. Nor did the cause have any bearing on the speed with which the flames spread. A fire might have started almost anywhere in the building—as a result of faulty wiring, careless disposal of cigarettes, or an accident in the kitchen—and still have caused a catastrophe of more or less the same awful proportions.

The responsibility for analyzing all phases of the fire rested with William Arthur Reilly, Boston's fire commissioner, and Stephen J. Garrity, the state fire marshal to whom Reilly reported. They were assisted by Fire Chief Pope and the heads of Fire Department divisions that had responded to the Grove alarms. These men had dealt with blazes in slums, warehouses, office buildings, and tenements for years. None of them had ever seen a fire that moved so fast, burned so fiercely, produced such curious gases, yet consumed so little of the building in which it broke out.

One purpose of Reilly's hearings had been to determine

the reason for the speed with which the terrible flames had moved, the composition of the materials they had fed upon, and the mysterious combination of chemical action and draught that had enabled the fire to travel through the air without any apparent dependence upon source or fuel.

Another question to be answered was why approximately half of the dead were unburned. Though their bodies were florid with the cherry-red of carbon monoxide poisoning, the speed with which they succumbed indicated that some other toxic material must have been produced in enormous volume during the brief fire.

In the course of his investigation, Reilly questioned experts from his own department, as well as patrons, employees, and victims of the fire. Now, to interpret the testimony, he obtained the advice of authorities on wiring, chemistry, fire control, and building construction.

State chemists who studied material consumed by the fire identified the presence of nitrous oxide in the fumes. This gas was produced from the burning of nitrous cellulose in the artificial leather.

In small doses the nitrous oxide produced sore throats. In larger amounts it caused a temporary loss of voice. Breathed in massive quantity it became the anaesthetic which caused so many in the Main Dining Room to lie down unconscious, later to die of carbon monoxide poisoning.

The medical examiners said there was "something deadly" in the fumes. But the bodies they examined were so heavily contaminated by carbon monoxide that no other possibly toxic materials could be found. Carbon monoxide certainly constitutes "something deadly," but many of the doctors were convinced that another gas—one more swiftly lethal—had to be involved.

Doctors Frank R. Dutra and Alan R. Moritz, of Harvard

Medical School, tested the leatherette that had burned in the Grove. They too detected the presence of various oxides of nitrogen in the fumes, but in small proportion. Much more significant, they believed, was the identification of a compound called acrolein, a derivative of glycerine. Acrolein fumes, they said, had caused the lesions in the respiratory tracts of victims. Those who succumbed to pulmonary oedema may have died because the lesions caused by the acrolein extended throughout their lungs.

Relatives of the badly burned dead took comfort from the medical opinion that few Grove victims suffered the terrible torture of burning alive. Post mortems suggested that most of such victims were already dead or mercifully unconscious when overtaken by fire. Those who suffered the worst were the ones who survived the fire but succumbed to their burns later in hospitals.

The testimony had also included many vivid personal accounts—such as one woman's impression that "the men went crazy in panic." But Reilly and Chief Pope were more interested in specific details that related to the fire itself.

For almost a year Reilly and Pope sifted through the outbursts of indignation, the accounts of emotional sensations, and the reports of escape. Finally, in November of 1943, they produced a sixty-four-page report containing their conclusions of what had happened on that tragic Saturday night.

In the analysis, Reilly said, "Plainly a large and extremely hot volume of burning material, largely gaseous in form, appeared at the top of the stairway leading from the Melody Lounge to the street floor within two to four minutes of the first appearance of flame in the basement room. The tangible material contained in that room, and actually burned, consisted principally of the cloth false ceiling, bamboo and rattan. Much of the cloth, rattan and bamboo contained in the Melody Lounge, and on the sides and lower walls of the stairway leading therefrom, was, in fact, not burned at all, and the same is true of the carpet on the stairway, contrary to all usual fire experience."

Reilly concluded that a major part of the tremendous volume of burning gas which forced its way to the first floor had consisted of carbon monoxide. A careful study of the size and construction of the Melody Lounge revealed conditions that were not only conducive to the production of partially burned gases, but would cause such gases to acquire unusual heat and pressure.

It was almost as though the Lounge had been diabolically designed to turn out poisons. Reilly's report outlined dispassionately the conditions that no one had suspected, no one had tried to change, and for which no one could be wholly blamed:

> The cloth false ceiling was tacked to wooden members attached to the underside of reinforced concrete beams in such a manner that there remained a dead space of sixteen inches between the actual ceiling and the false ceiling, with a deficiency of oxygen in this dead space.
>
> Under such conditions combustion of the cloth was incomplete, and occurred largely on its underside where oxygen was available.
>
> Products of such incomplete combustion, including monoxide, will themselves burn further as soon as additional oxygen is encountered. Furthermore, under the conditions prevailing in the basement room, there was no ready outlet for the heat generated by such partial combustion as took place. Such heat, therefore, increased both the temperature and the pressure of the partially burned gases, and acted to drive them forcefully to the nearest available outlet.

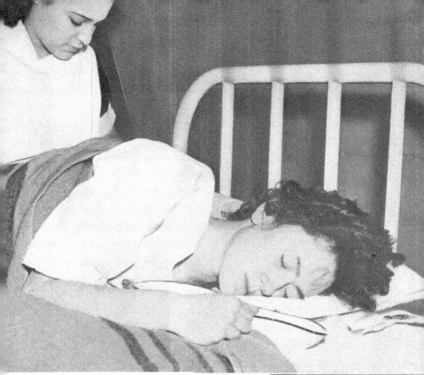

phie Urban, resting at City Hos-
al, wears on her forehead the
stick "M" indicating that she
eived an injection of morphine
on arrival.

ght) Clifford Johnson, whose re-
very from massive burns made
dical history, took his first ten-
ve steps in September, 1943. In
s, as in other ventures during
treatment, he was supported by
ses Adelena Kelly and Mercy
mith. (*Wide World photos*)

Barney Welansky, owner of the Cocoanut Grove arrives at Police Headquarters with a lawyer on each side. Welansky was indicted by the Grand Jury, convicted, and imprisoned as a result of the fire. (*Acme photo*)

Sixteen-year-old Stanley Tomaszewski, w h o s e match was thought to have started the fire, is seen here being sworn in before giving testimony at Fire Commissioner Reilly's official inquest. (*Wide World photo*)

The rapidity with which the partially burned gases moved from the basement room is indicated by the fact that many of the wooden strips upon which the cloth ceiling was tacked remained substantially untouched by the fire. Some of the cloth itself remained unburned. . . .

The fire did not burn itself out in the Melody Lounge primarily because in that confined space it lacked sufficient oxygen for complete combustion, and lacked also adequate means for dissipation of heat produced by the partial combustion which took place. Instead, it projected a large quantity of extremely hot, partially burned but still inflammable, gases toward and up the stairway.

Such a movement was accelerated by a cause independent of those already considered. Comparatively narrow (four (4) feet) and rising sharply, the stairway acted like a chimney, adding a draught of suction to the pressure generated in the room below by heat. Such effect appears to have been considerable, since it drew out the flame entirely, leaving unconsumed the wood and cloth material already referred to.

In the stairway itself a further acceleration of the process occurred. Here the partially burned hot gas was rapidly mixed and churned with considerable volume of air contained in the stairway itself. The further combustion resulting increased the temperature and rapidity of flow of the mass. I have already referred to the fact that much of the lower wall covering, and the carpeting, was unburned. This is a further indication of the high elevation of the fire and the rapidity of its flow.

The burning mass passed from the top of the stairway into a narrow connecting corridor and thence to the street floor foyer. The wall coverings of the foyer, consisting of artificial leather on cotton batting on concrete, did not withstand this blast of superheated burning gas. The burning and decomposition of such wall coverings, once again producing material largely gaseous, capable of further combustion and of very rapid movement, augmented the blast coming from the basement. Here again it is significant that much of this material on the lower part of the walls remained unburned.

At this point the only available direction of expansion for the hot, expanding mass was down the length of the foyer. Its progress in that direction appears to have been accelerated by a large ventilating exhaust fan placed over the further end on the Caricature Bar, acting to draw air from the foyer along the length of the room containing the Caricature Bar. Such fan had the effect of increasing the chimney effect of the stairway already referred to.

The great mass of compressed partially-burned gases spread at once into the Main Dining Room on the street floor of the first-class building, and into the Broadway Lounge on the street floor of the second-class building at 59 Broadway.

In the intense heat which resulted from the progress of the fire, decomposition of practically all combustible material in certain portions of the building resulted. In other sections little burning occurred and in these sections it is safe to assume the majority of persons who escaped were located.

If all the exits had been open, obviously more people would have got out of the building alive, and there would have been less retention of gases, heat and fire in the building. But even then many casualties would still have resulted, as fire and persons would still have had to rely upon the same means of egress.

Reilly estimated that it took from two to four minutes for the fire to develop momentum and cross the 43 feet of the Melody Lounge to the stairway. It raced down the 40-foot Foyer in seconds. For the total time from its appearance at the top of the stairs until it burst out of the distant Broadway Lounge doorway, 225 feet away, he estimated five minutes at most. Twelve minutes after the tree caught fire, everyone who was to die was dead or mortally burned.

Reilly's report dispelled a number of myths that had grown after the fire. One story that Reilly checked carefully was a rumour that the revolving door was equipped with a brake and could be stopped by a cashier if anyone tried to get out without paying. This was believed to be fact by several witnesses, but there was no truth in it.

An "eyewitness" from the Main Dining Room testified he saw the entire dance floor collapse, carrying with it hundreds who crashed down on top of those who were trapped in the Melody Lounge. The floor, of course, did not collapse; even if it had, it would not have crashed on the Melody Lounge, 150 feet away.

These misunderstandings were inevitable by-products of the passions aroused by the tragedy. Far more harmful, and totally unfair, were the distorted versions of the role played by Stanley Tomaszewski, the bar boy in the Melody Lounge. Such stories caused him to become the target of grief-stricken survivors. Many of them telephoned his home to call him "murderer," "defective delinquent," and "butcher."

One such call was taken by Stanley's mother, who was asked, "How does it feel to be the mother of a boy who has killed five hundred people?"

Some of the accusers even came to the house and made threats at the door. Others wrote vilifying letters. At one point, Stanley had to be taken into protective custody by the police. He was kept in a hotel under guard—but even this act was misunderstood, and tended to increase the aura of guilt around him.

Stanley had told his story under oath at both hearings. It was obvious that he had related as best he could exactly what had happened in the corner of the Melody Lounge. He was not sure whether he had stepped on the match, or had blown it out, but he was certain he had come out of the corner unaware that the fire had started, confident he had given the match his utmost care.

Maurice Levy's story supported this claim. Levy could not swear that he actually saw Stanley's match ignite the tree. All he could be certain of was that the fire had followed the lighting of the match.

So far as the official record was concerned, both Reilly and Garrity refused to place the blame on Stanley. A faulty electrical connection had been found directly behind the panelling in the corner where the fire commenced. It could easily have short-circuited, causing the fire.

Reilly's report exonerated the boy:

From all the evidence before me I am unable to determine the original cause or causes of the fire.

I find no evidence of incendiarism.

A bus boy, aged sixteen, employed by the Cocoanut Grove on the night of the fire, testified to lighting a match in the process of replacing an electric light bulb in the corner of the Melody Lounge, where the fire started, and dropping the match to the floor and stepping on it. After a careful study of all the evidence, and an analysis of all the facts presented before me, I am unable to find the conduct of this boy was the cause of the fire.

I have investigated and carefully considered, as possible causes of the fire, the following suggested possibilities: Alcoholic fumes, inflammable insecticides, motion picture film scraps, electric wiring, gasoline or fuel oil fumes, refrigerant gases, flame-proofing chemicals. There is no evidence before me to support a finding that any of these or any combination of them caused this fire.

This fire will be entered in the records of this department as being of unknown origin.

The public might accept the premise that the cause of the fire could not be proved, but it was nonetheless incensed at conditions in the Grove. Particularly appalling was the fact that every exit needed in the emergency had something wrong with it. The door at the top of the Melody Lounge stairway was locked; the Foyer's revolving door had jammed; the New Lounge door on Broadway opened inward, as did the double door on the Shawmut Street side of the Dining Room. Even the two doors leading to Shawmut Street from the basement were locked.

There was also a non-existent door eligible for blame—the steel fire door which had not yet been installed in the jamb provided for it between the Dining Room and the passageway to the New Lounge. But even if the door had been there, it would have shut automatically when fire reached it, thereby trapping those who fled from the Dining Room toward the New Lounge. The absent steel fire door would not necessarily have reduced the number of dead, but only changed their identity.

Except for the critical panic door, however, Reilly took a dim view of how the situation might have been altered if the other doors had been open:

I find that within two to five minutes of the first appearance of the fire most of the possible exits, including all exits normally open to the public, were useless. Pouring of fire through such exits made it impossible for humans to pass simultaneously through these exits safely. In the course of such pouring, the mass of burning gaseous material appears to have been depressed from its high elevation within the premises in order to pass through the exits. The finding of bodies piled up at many of the exits is attributable to this fact.

In almost any emergency involving a large number of people who must be evacuated, the critical factor is the control and prevention of panic. If panic can be averted, the toll of life usually can be held down.

The swiftness of the fire was so extreme that the time spent in organizing an orderly evacuation might have resulted in as many or more deaths than occurred. Speed thus became a prime requirement for survival, though by no means a guarantee. And the panic that resulted from speed was not a significant cause of death.

As it was, only about 220 patrons escaped unhurt. Waiters, bus boys, and musicians, because they knew the building intimately, fared far better than those who were in the club for the first time.

Dr. John W. Powell, a Maryland psychiatrist, studied all aspects of the Grove fire and classed it as one of the rare instances of true panic in the twentieth century.

22

WITHIN two days after he escaped from the jammed revolving door, Wilbur Boudrey developed
two distinct patches of white in his hair, permanent evidence that he had been one of the Grove's more
fortunate victims.

For months Helen Devine carried the complete outline of
a man's shoe across her breast, an injury sustained when she
was trampled upon getting out.

George Hayes began having nightmares in which he saw
the ever enlarging face of a frightened girl—the one he had
seen in the Foyer when he glanced back to plead with the
crowd to ease their pressure so he could move the revolving
door.

The aftermath of the Cocoanut Grove fire brought out
hundreds of stories such as these. There were tales also of
providential escapes.

A Watertown couple told of having gone to the Grove in a
party of six. The woman, who did not drink, ordered only
ginger ale. The others ordered mixed drinks. They were all
on the dance floor when the waiter brought to their table
a second round. The woman found that her first ginger ale,

from which she had taken only a few sips, had been replaced by a new one.

She became furious. Her husband explained that this was how night clubs made their money. But she was already incensed about having to pay fifty cents for plain ginger ale, and she said she would not stand for buying another one she didn't want. She insisted that they leave in protest.

The others in the party made little effort to conceal their annoyance with her. But they were not out of the club five minutes when it was swept by flames.

Lucky also was Dr. Vincent Sena, of Somerville, who made a special point, a few days after the fire, of visiting the nursery at Somerville Hospital. He went directly to a bassinet containing an infant born to Mrs. Elizabeth Zachel. Dr. Sena picked up the baby who, still unborn a few days before, had caused him distinct annoyance. The one night when he had hoped there would be no emergency calls—at least until the party was over—this thoughtless child had seen fit to enter the world.

Dr. Sena had been paged in the Grove's Main Dining Room at 9.30. When the fire broke out, he was safely at work in the maternity ward.

For each of such happy endings, there was a sad counterpart.

Somehow, word that the B.C. victory party had been cancelled did not reach the team's trainer, Larry Kenney. He and his wife, Marie, had arrived at the Grove early and asked for seats in the section on the Terrace which had been reserved for Boston College. When they were told that the party had been cancelled, they decided to stay anyway, on the chance that others would also show up despite the loss.

Larry's body was identified at Waterman's Funeral Home, and Marie's at the Southern Mortuary.

A special sadness seemed to surround the servicemen, some of whom had returned safely from battle overseas and were present in the Grove only by what afterwards appeared to have been a tragic wrenching of fate. There were 51 servicemen and two WACs dead—the figure included 17 from the Army, 26 Navy, 5 Coast Guardsmen, and 3 Marines.

Perhaps the highest price in grief was paid by Mrs. Mary Fitzgerald, seventy-one, of Wilmington. On the morning after the fire she sat by the window in her home, trying to hold back her emotions while one of her friends completed a series of telephone calls and two others offered comfort.

When the calls were completed, the woman was able to tell Mrs. Fitzgerald where each of her four sons was.

James was at Cambridge City Hospital, Harry was at Massachusetts General, and John and Wilfred were at Boston City. All four were dead.

Another woman lost a son for whom she had managed to save enough money for four years of college. She asked the Red Cross to help her find a survivor worthy of being given aid. They located a boy who had suffered a badly burned head. He became the woman's unofficially adopted son, and managed to stay on the Dean's List most of the way through college on the money she provided.

Three small children, the oldest of them only four, lost their mother, their father, an uncle, two aunts, and two grandparents in the fire.

A South Boston tavern owner, whose brother was a leader in the Massachusetts Democratic Party, lost a beautiful young daughter in the fire. He had been friendly with Maurice Tobin all during Tobin's meteoric rise in politics, but he placed the full blame for the conditions in the Grove on the handsome young mayor.

When Tobin called to pay his respects to the dead girl, the

tavern owner greeted him with a punch in the eye. A few days later, when both were attending another Cocoanut Grove funeral, the distraught father assaulted Tobin again, this time in full view of the mourners.

Among those people intimate with the Grove, the inquiry most often heard was, "How about Bunny?" Waiters, hat-check girls, musicians, and dancers wept openly when they learned that Bunny Leslie, the cigarette girl, had died. Vera Daniels, an employee who was hospitalized at Boston City, displayed such concern for Bunny during her own critical convalescence that the fact of Bunny's death was withheld from her for several weeks.

Bunny was also known and loved by people who worked in the motion picture film distributing district, where the Grove stood. She was probably the most widely mourned of all Grove casualties. Pepper Russell, the chorus girl, explained that Bunny's popularity stemmed from her sincere concern for the welfare of everyone she knew. There was also the fact that she was very pretty.

Bunny was a half sister to Lillian Roth, and very ambitious for a show business career of her own. She might have escaped the fire if this ambition had not led her to study the floor show every night from the Terrace, from which it was almost impossible to escape.

So staggering a death total, of course, could not be assuaged by the investigations, indictments, and trials alone. The tragedy stimulated action and change all over the nation.

Four days after the fire a party of workmen removed the two revolving doors from Boston City Hall. This was the first of a series of alterations undertaken as a result of the fire which eventually affected every public building in the Commonwealth of Massachusetts.

It was made law that all egress doors in buildings used by the public must open outward. If the owner of a building wanted a revolving door, he could have it, but it had to be flanked by at least two doors that could be opened by pushing on a bar or plate. Thus it seemed unusual only to outsiders when Boston's Statler Hotel fourteen years later, installed a series of spacious revolving doors above each of which was lettered, "Not an Accredited Egress Door."

The full panic in the Cocoanut Grove had not occurred until the lights went out. The image of hundreds of terror-stricken men and women struggling helplessly in the darkness resulted in legislation in many states—legislation which made mandatory the installation of emergency lighting in public buildings. In Boston this emergency equipment had to be independent of any remote power source, and had to turn on automatically. Years later, when an Ed Sullivan stage show originated from the Boston Opera House, a power failure blacked out the city. The entire centre orchestra was occupied by paraplegics from a veterans' hospital. These invalids were protected from panic by a bank of emergency lights in whose yellow glow comedian Victor Borge entertained for nearly an hour while power was being restored.

Another Massachusetts law forbade the setting up of a live Christmas tree anywhere in a public building, even if located under ceiling sprinklers.

Fire codes all over the nation were revised in terms of what had been learned from the Cocoanut Grove. In the days immediately following the disaster, fire chiefs from cities and towns in many parts of the country came to Boston to study the ruins, and to take back to their communities the knowledge they acquired.

Inflammable decorations have since been outlawed in nearly every American community. The building codes in

New York, Chicago, Indianapolis, and many other large cities have been revamped in accordance with knowledge gained from the fire. New York's code for hotels actually cites the Cocoanut Grove fire as the reason for some of its provisions.

The insurance companies, too, learned costly lessons from the tragedy. No insurance inspector had even visited the Grove for more than a year before it burned, despite the knowledge of the insuring company that new work was being done on the premises. The Grove had apparently been considered an excellent risk, for the rate paid to insure the building against first was only 17.1 cents per hundred dollars, as against a base rate of 26 cents per hundred generally applied in Boston. Thereafter, the rates on all such buildings were set according to radically revised standards, and regular safety inspections were required.

Private insurance firms estimated that they paid about two million dollars to beneficiaries of Grove victims, in addition to the $80,000 in fire insurance on the Grove and its contents. These firms now began to take a more diligent view of their double-indemnity clauses.

In 1945, almost three years after the fire, the Cocoanut Grove suddenly produced a startling news story.

On June 22, expert safe-crackers broke into the walled-up shell of the building and descended to a section of the basement that was so cleverly concealed it had not been located during any of the probes that followed the fire.

The burglars penetrated a section of the wall containing a large vault, which they blasted open. Police found nothing in the vault when they investigated. The Welanskys said they had no knowledge of the existence of the old safe.

It was speculated that some old crony of the Grove's first

owner, King Solomon—possibly one who had been in prison until then—had finally learned where some of Solomon's bootleg loot was hidden and had come to retrieve it before the building was torn down.

In this story, as in almost every news report from the Cocoanut Grove, different death tolls were recalled by various newspapers. The figure seemed to fluctuate according to the whim of whoever was writing the story. Ultimately the figure settled at 492.

But Fire Commissioner Reilly's report on the fire, published November 19, 1943, carried an alphabetical list of both dead and injured. Labelled "Master List," and carrying the note, "As of December 10, 1942, and adjusted to October 16, 1943," it claimed to cancel and supersede all others.

This list numbered 489 as dead and 166 as treated in hospitals. But it did not include patients treated and immediately released, or servicemen admitted to military hospitals. Nor did it contain the name "Eleanor B. Powerell," listed at City Hospital as having died there. There were several other discrepancies between the Master List and the sources from which it was compiled. These might account for the idea that 492 died, when, in fact, only 490 deaths can be verified.

Whatever may have been the true total of deaths in the Cocoanut Grove fire, it was the worst disaster of its kind in history. The arrival of dead and injured at City Hospital alone occurred at a faster rate than that experienced by any London hospital during the Blitz.

It should be noted that Boston City Hospital, like most municipal institutions, had always been an object of criticism. It wasn't the kind of hospital that many people went to by choice, unless they were fortunate enough to know of the skills and knowledge available there.

But on the night of the Cocoanut Grove fire, City Hospital received and treated more patients than all of the others combined. The most urgent, and consequently most hopeless, cases were sent there. If more than half of these victims had died because of lack of immediate attention it would not have been surprising.

But this did not happen. The death toll at Boston City was only four per cent higher than at Massachusetts General, where far fewer victims were received.

Boston City Hospital emerged from the Cocoanut Grove disaster in pure glory, as any of its surviving Grove patients will gratefully attest.

Massachusetts General Hospital, which also performed magnificently during the crisis, later compiled the papers written by its doctors. These were published in a volume covering all aspects of treatment to Cocoanut Grove patients. The book became a standard medical text.

One of the most unusual publications resulting from the fire was a painstaking survey by Dr. Maxwell Finland, of City Hospital. Most of the Cocoanut Grove deaths, even in some of the cases where burns were massive and severe, were caused by asphyxia resulting either directly from the fumes inhaled or later by the oedema they caused.

Dr. Finland literally walked miles through Boston City Hospital to obtain his data. He interviewed seventy-two of the surviving patients. In addition, he was able to acquire second-hand information concerning several others.

What he wanted to know from the patients was where they had been sitting, in what direction they had moved, and whether they had known where they were when they lost consciousness.

From these stories, Finland pieced together an elaborate diagram on a floor plan of the Grove. The location of each patron was indicated, and arrows showed the direction in which each had moved. The diagram further indicated whether or not the patient lost consciousness inside the club.

Accompanying the diagram was a brief synopsis of every patient's recollections, his condition on arrival at the hospital, and a comparison between the extent of his burns and the degree of his respiratory damage.

Finland acknowledged in his report that his data were necessarily crude, for they were based on the recollections of people who had been in terror when fleeing the Grove, and in pain or discomfort when interviewed. Furthermore, the cases which could have provided the most revealing information were those from whom it could never be obtained— those who suffered such massive respiratory damage that they died.

But the diagram showed quite conclusively that it didn't much matter where a person was sitting in the Cocoanut Grove that night; the poison was everywhere, and if he had not been lucky enough to escape in the first few minutes, a patient was certain to have inhaled some of it. There was no apparent ratio between those sitting in one place and those in another as to whether they received burns, or poison, or both. The charts showed that it had been an erratic, capricious fire which might kill one person and spare the one beside him.

The diagram clearly reflected another strange aspect of the tragedy; scores of patrons had actually stopped at the cloakrooms, thinking there was time enough for them to get their coats and furs before fleeing the fire.

One puzzling story conflicted with Dr. Finland's chart. It was given in testimony by George Hayes, the second man to escape through the revolving door in the Foyer.

Hayes' story was corroborated by his wife, and by Mrs. Boudrey and Catherine Fallon, all of whom had stood together under the stucco archway and watched what occurred.

They insisted that only four people came through the revolving door alive: Boudrey, Hayes, the bond saleswoman whose dress was afire, and an Army officer who followed her.

Furthermore, Hayes testified, he and his party continued to watch the doorway until they saw it fill with flame which shot far out over Piedmont Street. They stayed there until firemen began evacuating bodies.

No one who came through the revolving door has any explanation for the apparent contradiction. Some of those who told Finland they came through that door may have meant that they were carried through by rescuers after the fire had been controlled.

One such victim was Martin Sheridan, the reporter who had accompanied Buck Jones. He was unconscious and had no idea who had carried him to safety.

But two years later, after considerable surgery and convalescence, Sheridan was far out in the Pacific aboard the U.S.S. *Fremont*, an amphibious group flagship from which he was covering the occupation of Ulithi Atoll in the Caroline Islands. He was waiting for a movie to be shown on deck one night when a seaman approached him and said, "Aren't you Martin Sheridan?"

"That's right," said the reporter.

"Well, I'm the fellow who pulled you out of the Cocoanut Grove fire."

All Sheridan could say was "Thank you—thank you!"

The sailor told him his name, Howard E. Sotherden, and that he was from Tiverton, Rhode Island. He had been in Boston on a week-end liberty the night of the Grove fire.

When he first heard the sirens, he flagged a cab and rode

as far as Tremont and Broadway. Then he ran to the Grove, where firemen were soaking down the Piedmont Street entrance.

Sotherden ran through the steaming, smouldering Foyer, then struggled over charred bodies, hose line, and broken furniture until he reached the Terrace. There he stepped on a form which responded to his touch. He dragged the victim toward the Foyer, and turned him over to other rescuers. He went back a second time and pulled another victim out of the debris. Outside he took a look at the man. His hair was singed short, his face was smudged with dirt and soot, and a pair of broken glasses hung down from one ear. Sotherden heard two nearby newspapermen exclaim, "That's Marty Sheridan!"

The name meant nothing to Sotherden, who went back in and helped carry out two more victims, both dead. But when he heard that Sheridan was aboard the *Fremont*, he recognized the name immediately.

Sheridan wired the strange story to the Boston *Globe*, and later sent a copy of it to Secretary of the Navy James Forrestal. It was the first notice the Navy had received of Sotherden's heroism, and he was awarded a special citation.

In August of 1945, a gang of workmen arrived on Piedmont Street to begin razing the remains of the building which once had been known as the Cocoanut Grove.

First they tore down the tall, weathered, board fence that had been put up against the walls after the fire. Then a party of workers entered the building to determine the best method of demolishing the charred shell.

As they walked through the dark, echoing rooms, their flashlights illuminated articles among the old debris. A woman's wrist watch, blackened by fire, was found first.

Someone picked up an empty wallet. Another discovered a stub from a ticket to the Boston College-Holy Cross game.

The only reminder that the doomed building had once been a night club was found in the passageway leading from the stage to the Shawmut Street exit.

It was the piano score from an orchestration of a tune popular in November, 1942—"This Is My Last Affair."

ACKNOWLEDGMENTS

RESEARCHING a subject with as many ramifications as the Cocoanut Grove fire could never be done without the friendly co-operation of hundreds of people. To acknowledge the specific contribution of each would be impossible: sometimes one piece of information led to another and only the third belonged in this book. So I shall try, instead, to outline the sources from which material was obtained, and leave the reader to realize how much effort had to be expended by generous people who had nothing to gain except the anticipated satisfaction of seeing the entire story set forth in one place.

Although I work for the Boston *Globe*, the other Boston newspapers offered the use of their photographs and files. Reporters and photographers who covered the event supplied innumerable details and sources that I could never have discovered on my own.

Officials of the Boston Fire Department, the Police Department, the Building and other municipal departments, made available without exception the records, transcripts, diagrams, photographs, and miscellaneous documents important to the story. The Massachusetts Department of Public Safety also offered its facilities and records, tolerating my presence there for several months.

Doctors, nurses, administrative personnel, and staff members of the hospitals involved withstood my bothersome probings without complaint. None of them ever asked how the material would be used, or expressed reticence in revealing facts which could easily have been withheld.

Although it cost them recollections of grief and pain, many of the people mentioned in this book told me their stories freely.

In the course of my research, it soon became apparent that the Cocoanut Grove fire was a tragedy which still holds a grip on thousands of people in the Boston area. I met no one who was immune to the suffering created that night.

Try as I did, I found it impossible to pursue the story without identifying with the pain and heartbreak inflicted on Grove victims. My feelings, naturally, have crept into this book, but I hope no one will suspect me of having tried to pretend that I was there. I was not, and if the story told in this book remains vivid, it is because those who were there can never forget.

Postscript

As with all tragedies such as the fire in the Cocoanut Grove night-club, the nation was gripped by the revelations unearthed in the investigation which followed. The decorative cloth used for wall coverings, which had been approved based on tests for common sources of ignition such as matches and cigarettes, was purportedly treated with fire retardant ammonium sulfate upon installation, but there was no documentation that the treatment was maintained at the required intervals. The air-conditioning freon refrigerant had been replaced with the flammable gas methyl chloride because of a wartime shortage. It was determined that the fire was initiated by an electrical short and fueled by the methyl chloride in the air conditioning unit. The Boston Fire Department report of seventy pages issued almost a year to the day of the fire attributed the rapid, gaseous spread of the fire to a buildup of carbon monoxide gas from oxygen-deprived combustion in the enclosed space above the false ceiling of the Melody Lounge. The gas exuded from enclosed spaces as its temperature rose and ignited rapidly as it mixed with oxygen above the entryway, up the stairway to the main floor, and along ceilings. The fire accelerated as the stairway created a thermal draft, and the high-temperature gas fire ignited the pyroxylin (leatherette) wall and ceiling covering in the foyer, which in turn exuded flammable gas. The report also documented the fire safety code violations and door designs that contributed to the large loss of life.

Reforms have followed the fire, not only in Boston but across the nation. Massachusetts and other states enacted laws for public establishments banning flammable decorations and inward-swinging exit doors, and requiring exit signs to be visible at all times (meaning that the exit signs had to have independent sources of electricity and be easily readable in even the thickest smoke). The new laws also required that revolving doors used for egress must either be flanked by at least one normal, outward-swinging door or retrofitted to permit the individual door leaves to fold flat, permitting traffic in a panic situation, and further required that no emergency exits be chained or bolted shut in such a way as to bar escape through the doors during a panic or emergency. Commissions were established by several states that would levy heavy fines or even shut down establishments for infractions of any of these laws. These later became the basis for several federal fire laws and code restrictions placed on nightclubs, theaters, banks, public buildings, and restaurants across the nation. It also led to the formation of several national organizations dedicated to fire safety.

The fire also resulted in new ways of caring for both burns and smoke inhalation. Burn victims suffer both from impaired breathing from inhaling extremely hot, often toxic, air, as well as from infection of the burn areas. A more targeted regimen of fluid therapy to combat tracheobronchitis was developed, along with the use of antibiotics; a gauze treatment of petroleum jelly and boric acid replaced tannic acid as a more effective way to combat infection. The use of skin grafts and specialized burn units was also developed. The tragedy initiated serious research into post-traumatic stress disorder.

Where are they today? Barney Welansky was convicted on nineteen counts of manslaughter and served four years of a 12 to 15-year sentence before being pardoned by Massachusetts governor Maurice Tobin, who, as mayor of Boston at the time of the fire, barely escaped indictment himself; Welansky died of cancer nine months after his release. Stanley Tomaszewki graduated from Boston College and became a federal auditor; dying at the age of 68 in 1994. As for the nightclub on Piedmont Street, after being torn down in 1945 it became a parking lot before urban renewal radically changed the area; today much of the club's footprint lies under the Revere Hotel, with the rest of 25 Piedmont Street built up as condominiums. A memorial plaque was installed on the sidewalk near the site in 1993. The Boston Licensing Board ruled that no establishment in the city could ever again be a "Cocoanut Grove," relegating the name forever to Boston's past.

Index

248

www.ingramcontent.com/pod-product-compliance
Ingram Content Group UK Ltd.
Pitfield, Milton Keynes, MK11 3LW, UK
UKHW051231030125
3930UKWH00072B/474

9 781648 373411